The Lost Kingdoms of Syria

Copyright © 2023 by Amira Bakri-Jung and Einar Felix Hansen.

All rights reserved. No part of this publication may be reproduced, stored in a retrieval system, or transmitted, in any form or by any means, electronic, mechanical, photocopying, recording, or otherwise, without the prior written permission of the copyright holder. This book was created with the help of Artificial Intelligence technology.

The contents of this book are intended for entertainment purposes only. While every effort has been made to ensure the accuracy and reliability of the information presented, the author and publisher make no warranties or representations as to the accuracy, completeness, or suitability of the information contained herein. The information presented in this book is not intended as a substitute for professional advice, and readers should consult with qualified professionals in the relevant fields for specific advice.

The Land of Ancient Civilizations 6

Syria's Earliest Inhabitants 11

Tracing the Origins of Syrian Culture 14

The Birth of Urban Centers 17

The Rise of Ebla: Trade and Diplomacy 20

Kingdoms and Empires: From Mari to Ugarit 23

The Hittite Influence on Syria 26

The Aramaeans: Nomads to Settlers 29

Assyrian Dominance and Resistance 32

The Neo-Babylonian and Persian Rule 35

Alexander the Great and Hellenistic Syria 38

The Seleucid Dynasty: Greek and Persian Fusion 41

Palmyra: Queen of the Syrian Desert 44

The Roman Conquest and Pax Romana 47

Christianity Takes Root in Syria 50

Byzantine Syria: Center of Christian Civilization 53

The Muslim Conquest: Damascus and the Umayyads 56

The Abbasid Era: Intellectual and Cultural Flourishing 59

The Crusaders and the Kingdom of Jerusalem 62

The Ayyubids: Salahuddin and the Reconquest 65

The Mamluk Rule: Power Struggles and Stability 68

Ottoman Syria: Prosperity and Decline 71

Lawrence of Arabia and the Arab Revolt 74

Syria under French Mandate: Colonial Struggles 77

Independence and the Founding of Modern Syria 80

United Arab Republic and Political Transformations 84

The Ba'ath Party and Hafez al-Assad's Rule 87

Contemporary Syria: Bashar al-Assad and the Arab Spring 90

Ancient Treasures: Animals of Syria 93

Exploring Historic Sites: UNESCO World Heritage 96

Iconic Cities: Damascus, Aleppo, and Homs 99

Palmyra: A Jewel of the Desert 102

Syria Today: Challenges and Hopes for the Future 105

Conclusion 109

The Land of Ancient Civilizations

In the vast expanse of the Middle East, nestled between the Taurus Mountains and the Arabian Desert, lies a land that has witnessed the rise and fall of countless civilizations throughout its long and storied history. This land, known today as Syria, holds within its borders the remnants of ancient civilizations that have left an indelible mark on the development of human culture and society.

Stretching back to the dawn of civilization, Syria's fertile plains and strategic location made it an attractive destination for early settlers. Archaeological evidence suggests that as early as the 10th millennium BCE, hunter-gatherer communities began to settle in the region, transitioning to a sedentary way of life and laying the foundations for agricultural practices.

One of the earliest known civilizations to emerge in Syria was that of Ebla, a kingdom that flourished around the third millennium BCE. Located in modern-day Tell Mardikh, Ebla reached its zenith during the 24th century BCE. It boasted an advanced system of governance and administration, with its capital serving as a major trade hub, connecting Mesopotamia with the Mediterranean.

As Ebla declined, other kingdoms rose to prominence in Syria. Mari, situated along the Euphrates River, became a thriving center of trade and culture during the early second millennium BCE. The city flourished under the reign of King Zimri-Lim, whose extensive correspondence with other rulers of the time provides invaluable insights into the political and social dynamics of the era.

During the Late Bronze Age, Syria witnessed the rise of the Hittites, an Anatolian civilization that exerted its influence over the region. The Hittites established their capital at Hattusa (present-day Boğazkale, Turkey), but their presence and dominance extended into the northern reaches of Syria. The Hittite Empire, known for its military might and administrative prowess, played a significant role in shaping the political landscape of the Near East.

Around the 12th century BCE, a group of Semitic-speaking peoples known as the Aramaeans began to migrate into Syria, eventually establishing their own kingdoms. The Aramaeans were a nomadic people who gradually transitioned into settled societies, adapting to the political and cultural traditions of the region. They contributed to the spread of the Aramaic language, which became widely used as a lingua franca throughout the Near East.

The ancient Assyrians, known for their military conquests and imperial ambitions, brought Syria under their control during the 9th century BCE. Under the rule of powerful Assyrian kings such as Tiglath-Pileser III and Sargon II, Syria became an integral part of the mighty Neo-Assyrian Empire. The Assyrians left their mark through their military campaigns, administrative systems, and cultural assimilation of conquered territories.

The balance of power in Syria shifted once again with the rise of the Babylonian Empire in the 7th century BCE. Led by King Nebuchadnezzar II, the Babylonians defeated the Assyrians and established their dominance over the region. Syria, including the city of Damascus, fell under Babylonian control and became an important center for trade and cultural exchange.

In the wake of the Persian conquest led by Cyrus the Great in the 6th century BCE, Syria became a satrapy within the vast Achaemenid Empire. The Persians, known for their tolerance and efficient administration, fostered economic growth and encouraged the development of local traditions. The Persian influence in Syria laid the groundwork for the subsequent Hellenistic period.

The arrival of Alexander the Great in the 4th century BCE marked a significant turning point in Syria's history. The Macedonian conqueror swept through the region, dismantling the Persian Empire and establishing his own Hellenistic empire. The city of Damascus, in particular, played a crucial role in Alexander's campaigns and became a prominent Greek polis, blending Greek and local cultures.

Following Alexander's death, the Seleucid Dynasty emerged as the ruling power in Syria. The Seleucids, founded by Seleucus I Nicator, created a vast empire that encompassed much of the eastern Mediterranean and Mesopotamia. The Seleucid period witnessed a rich fusion of Greek and Near Eastern traditions, with major cities like Antioch becoming centers of Hellenistic culture and learning.

During the 1st century BCE, Palmyra, an oasis city in the Syrian Desert, rose to prominence as a key trading hub along the Silk Road. The Palmyrene Empire, led by the powerful queen Zenobia, briefly challenged Roman authority and established a prosperous and cosmopolitan city. Palmyra's ruins stand as a testament to its former grandeur and its unique blend of Roman, Greek, and local influences.

With the Roman conquest of Syria in the 1st century BCE, the region became an integral part of the Roman Empire. Roman rule brought stability, infrastructure development, and the spread of Roman culture throughout the region. Cities like Damascus, Bosra, and Apamea thrived under Roman administration, showcasing the impressive architectural achievements and cultural diversity of the time.

The rise of Christianity in the 1st century CE had a profound impact on Syria. The city of Antioch, one of the early centers of Christian activity, played a pivotal role in the spread of the new faith. Important figures such as Paul the Apostle and Ignatius of Antioch were associated with Antioch, which became a vital early Christian community.

With the fall of the Western Roman Empire in the 5th century CE, Syria came under Byzantine rule. The Byzantine period saw the consolidation of Christianity as the dominant religion, with the construction of numerous churches and monastic complexes. Byzantine Syria witnessed a flourishing of artistic and intellectual pursuits, leaving behind magnificent mosaics and religious manuscripts.

The Muslim conquest of Syria in the 7th century CE brought about a significant cultural and religious transformation. Led by the Rashidun Caliphate, Islamic armies overcame Byzantine resistance and established the city of Damascus as the capital of the new Umayyad Caliphate. Damascus became a vibrant center of Islamic civilization, known for its architectural masterpieces such as the Umayyad Mosque.

As the centuries passed, Syria experienced subsequent periods of foreign rule, including the Crusader states and the Mongol invasions. The Ottoman Empire, which emerged in the 14th century CE, brought Syria under its dominion for several centuries. Ottoman rule brought stability and economic prosperity to some regions of Syria, but also entailed occasional periods of unrest and uprisings.

In the early 20th century, following the collapse of the Ottoman Empire, Syria emerged as a French Mandate territory. The French colonial administration, which lasted until the mid-20th century, led to tensions and nationalist movements seeking independence. Syria eventually gained its sovereignty in 1946, ushering in a new era of self-governance.

The ancient civilizations that flourished in Syria have left an enduring legacy in the region. Today, the archaeological sites, historical monuments, and cultural heritage of ancient Syria stand as a testament to the rich and diverse history that unfolded within its borders. The land of ancient civilizations continues to captivate and inspire, inviting visitors to explore its past and embrace its vibrant present.

Syria's Earliest Inhabitants

The ancient land of Syria has been home to human civilizations for thousands of years. As we delve into the depths of history, we encounter the earliest inhabitants who laid the foundation for the rich tapestry of Syrian culture and heritage.

Archaeological evidence suggests that as early as the Paleolithic period, around 1.2 million years ago, human presence can be traced in what is now Syria. Stone tools, such as handaxes and scrapers, discovered at sites like Dederiyeh Cave and Afrin Basin, provide insights into the hunting and gathering lifestyle of these early inhabitants.

During the Neolithic period, around 10,000 BCE, the shift from a nomadic existence to settled farming communities took place in Syria. Excavations at sites like Tell Abu Hureyra and Tell Ramad have revealed evidence of early agriculture, including the cultivation of wheat, barley, and legumes. Domestication of animals, such as goats and sheep, played a crucial role in the transition to an agrarian society.

The development of agriculture led to the establishment of permanent settlements and the emergence of complex social structures. Sites like Jerf el-Ahmar and Tell Aswad provide glimpses into the early Neolithic villages, featuring circular or rectangular houses made of mud-brick and evidence of communal activities, such as food storage and ritual practices.

As the Neolithic period progressed, these early communities experienced cultural advancements. The invention of pottery, witnessed at sites like Mureybet and Tell Sabi Abyad, revolutionized the storage and preparation of food. Intricate pottery vessels with elaborate designs reflect the artistic abilities and aesthetic sensibilities of these ancient inhabitants.

The late Neolithic period saw the rise of larger, more complex settlements in Syria. Excavations at sites like Tell Halula and Tell Brak reveal evidence of urban planning and the emergence of specialized labor, including craft production. The appearance of temples, monumental architecture, and evidence of long-distance trade indicate the development of complex societies with hierarchical structures.

Around 3000 BCE, the Chalcolithic period brought further cultural and technological advancements to Syria. The discovery of copper artifacts, such as jewelry and tools, at sites like Tell Khalaf and Tell Abu Hureyra, attests to the mastery of metallurgy by these ancient inhabitants. The utilization of copper in weaponry, agricultural tools, and decorative objects points to the increasing complexity of their society.

During the Bronze Age, spanning from approximately 3000 to 1200 BCE, Syria witnessed the rise of urban centers and the emergence of powerful city-states. Ebla, one of the most notable city-states, reached its peak during the mid-third millennium BCE. Excavations at the site have uncovered an extensive palace complex, an archive of cuneiform tablets, and evidence of a sophisticated administrative system.

Other prominent Bronze Age city-states in Syria include Mari, located along the Euphrates River, and Ugarit, situated on the Mediterranean coast. These cities flourished as economic and cultural hubs, engaging in long-distance trade with neighboring regions and showcasing vibrant artistic traditions. The discovery of elaborate royal tombs, impressive city walls, and religious structures highlights the achievements of these early urban civilizations.

The transition from the Bronze Age to the Iron Age brought significant changes to Syria. Around 1200 BCE, the region witnessed a period of turmoil and upheaval, often referred to as the Late Bronze Age collapse. The fall of many city-states and the arrival of new populations, such as the Aramaeans, marked a transitional phase in the region's history.

The ancient inhabitants of Syria, from the Paleolithic to the Iron Age, laid the foundation for the diverse and resilient civilizations that would follow. Their innovations in agriculture, pottery, metallurgy, and urban planning paved the way for future cultural achievements. The remnants of their settlements, artifacts, and cultural practices provide glimpses into their lives and contribute to our understanding of the rich tapestry of Syrian history.

Tracing the Origins of Syrian Culture

The origins of Syrian culture can be traced back to the ancient civilizations that flourished in the region. Through the exploration of archaeological sites, artifacts, and historical records, we can unravel the multifaceted layers of cultural development that have shaped Syria's rich heritage.

One of the earliest influences on Syrian culture can be attributed to the indigenous peoples who inhabited the region during prehistoric times. These early inhabitants, dating back to the Paleolithic and Neolithic periods, developed a distinct way of life based on hunting, gathering, and eventually, settled farming communities. Their knowledge of agriculture, pottery-making, and early forms of art laid the groundwork for the cultural traditions that would evolve in Syria.

As the centuries passed, Syria became a crossroads of civilizations, attracting various external influences. The region's strategic location, connecting the Mediterranean with Mesopotamia and Anatolia, facilitated the exchange of ideas, goods, and cultural practices.

One of the most influential civilizations that left a lasting impact on Syrian culture was that of the ancient Mesopotamians. The city-states of Ebla and Mari, located in present-day Syria, were key players in the trade networks that connected Mesopotamia with the Mediterranean. As a result, cultural exchange and the adoption of Mesopotamian customs, such as cuneiform writing, religious beliefs, and administrative systems, shaped the early development of Syrian culture.

Another significant cultural influence on Syria came from the ancient Egyptians. Trade relations between Egypt and the Levant fostered the transfer of goods, ideas, and artistic styles. Egyptian influence can be seen in the artistic motifs found in Syrian pottery, as well as in the adoption of certain religious beliefs and practices.

The Hittites, an Anatolian civilization, exerted their influence over parts of Syria during the Late Bronze Age. This led to a blending of Hittite and indigenous cultures, particularly in the northern regions of Syria. The Hittite impact can be observed in architectural styles, artistic representations, and the adoption of certain religious and political practices.

During the Iron Age, the Assyrians and Babylonians played a significant role in shaping Syrian culture. The Assyrians, known for their military might, imposed their rule over Syria, leaving behind traces of their influence in administrative practices, art, and architecture. Similarly, the Babylonians, through their conquests and cultural exchanges, left an indelible mark on Syrian society.

The ancient Greeks, under the leadership of Alexander the Great, brought Hellenistic influence to Syria. The city of Antioch, founded by Seleucus I Nicator, became a prominent Hellenistic center, blending Greek and local cultures. Greek art, architecture, and philosophical ideas found expression in Antioch and other urban centers, contributing to the cosmopolitan nature of Syrian culture.

With the advent of Roman rule in the 1st century BCE, Syria experienced further cultural assimilation and transformation. Roman influence can be seen in the architectural marvels of cities like Palmyra, Damascus, and

Bosra, where Roman engineering and urban planning techniques were employed. The spread of Roman customs, language, and legal systems also left a lasting impact on Syrian society.

The arrival of Christianity in the 1st century CE brought yet another layer of cultural significance to Syria. The region became a cradle of early Christian activity, with Antioch emerging as an important center for the burgeoning faith. Prominent figures such as Paul the Apostle and Ignatius of Antioch contributed to the development of Christian theology and ecclesiastical traditions in Syria.

Over the centuries, successive waves of migration, conquest, and cultural exchange continued to shape Syrian culture. The Arab-Islamic conquest in the 7th century CE introduced Islam and Arab traditions, influencing the language, religion, and societal norms of the region. The Crusader period and subsequent Mamluk and Ottoman rule also left their mark on Syrian culture, with the incorporation of European architectural styles, artistic techniques, and culinary influences.

Today, Syrian culture is a rich tapestry that reflects the diverse historical influences and contributions of various civilizations. From the ancient indigenous peoples to the interactions with Mesopotamians, Egyptians, Hittites, Greeks, Romans, and others, Syrian culture has evolved into a unique blend of traditions, languages, cuisine, and artistic expressions. Exploring the origins of Syrian culture allows us to appreciate the depth and resilience of a heritage shaped by millennia of cultural exchange and historical crossroads.

The Birth of Urban Centers

The birth of urban centers in the ancient land of Syria marks a significant milestone in human civilization. As societies transitioned from nomadic lifestyles to settled agricultural communities, the development of urban centers became a defining characteristic of social, economic, and cultural progress.

The earliest urban centers in Syria emerged during the Neolithic period, around 10,000 BCE. As agricultural practices advanced and communities became more sedentary, the need for centralized settlements arose. These early urban centers served as hubs for trade, social interaction, and communal activities.

One notable example of an early urban center in Syria is Jericho, located near the modern-day Syrian border. Dating back to around 9000 BCE, Jericho is considered one of the oldest continuously inhabited cities in the world. Excavations at the site have revealed evidence of complex structures, defensive walls, and an organized urban layout, providing insights into the early stages of urban development.

As the Neolithic period progressed, larger and more sophisticated urban centers began to emerge. Catalhoyuk, located in present-day Turkey but influenced the surrounding regions, including Syria, is a prime example. Flourishing between 7500 and 5700 BCE, Catalhoyuk boasted a dense population and intricate urban planning. The houses, built closely together and interconnected, featured elaborate wall paintings and evidence of social differentiation within the community.

Moving into the Bronze Age, urbanization gained further momentum in Syria. The city of Ebla, which thrived between 2500 and 2250 BCE, stands as a remarkable testament to the birth of urban centers in the region. Ebla's strategic location near major trade routes facilitated its rise as a prominent economic and cultural hub. The city featured a centralized administrative system, impressive palaces, and a vast archive of cuneiform tablets, shedding light on its complex societal structure.

Another significant urban center during the Bronze Age was Mari, situated along the Euphrates River. Flourishing from the 3rd to the early 2nd millennium BCE, Mari played a crucial role in regional trade and diplomacy. Excavations at the site have uncovered a well-organized city layout, a grand palace complex, and evidence of international connections through its extensive archives.

The Iron Age witnessed the consolidation of urban centers in Syria. One remarkable example is the city of Damascus, which has a history dating back over 5,000 years. Damascus served as an important commercial and cultural center, positioned along major trade routes between Mesopotamia, Anatolia, and Egypt. Its strategic location and sophisticated urban planning contributed to its significance as a vibrant urban hub.

During the Hellenistic period, the city of Antioch, founded by Seleucus I Nicator, emerged as a major urban center. Antioch became a cosmopolitan city, blending Greek, Roman, and local cultures. It boasted impressive architectural achievements, such as the famous Roman aqueduct, theaters, and public spaces that showcased the grandeur of Hellenistic urban planning.

Roman rule further solidified the urban landscape in Syria. Cities like Palmyra, Apamea, and Bosra flourished as Roman colonies, reflecting the sophistication of Roman urban design and architectural marvels. The integration of Roman infrastructure, including roads, aqueducts, and public buildings, elevated the quality of life and the social fabric of these urban centers.

The birth of urban centers in Syria was not solely limited to political and economic aspects. These cities also served as centers of cultural exchange and intellectual flourishing. Libraries, academies, and centers of learning emerged, attracting scholars, philosophers, and artists from diverse backgrounds.

The birth of urban centers in Syria marked a transformative period in human history, shaping the trajectory of civilization in the region. From the early settlements of the Neolithic period to the grandeur of the Roman cities, the development of urban centers in Syria reflected the ingenuity, social organization, and cultural achievements of ancient societies. Exploring the birth of urban centers allows us to appreciate the foundational role these cities played in shaping the cultural heritage and legacy of Syria.

The Rise of Ebla: Trade and Diplomacy

The rise of Ebla during the third millennium BCE marked a significant period in the history of Syria. Situated in present-day Tell Mardikh, Ebla emerged as a thriving kingdom known for its extensive trade networks and diplomatic prowess. The kingdom's prominence was shaped by its strategic location, economic resources, and administrative capabilities.

Ebla reached its zenith during the mid-third millennium BCE, particularly under the rule of King Ibbit-Lim. The city became a bustling center of commerce, attracting traders and merchants from distant lands. Ebla's location between Mesopotamia and the Mediterranean coast made it a crucial link in the transregional trade routes of the time. The city's commercial success can be attributed to its control over key trade routes, such as the Royal Road, which connected it with other city-states and regions.

Ebla's prosperity was fueled by its access to valuable resources, including timber, metals, textiles, and agricultural products. The kingdom's agricultural practices, such as extensive irrigation systems, enabled the cultivation of a variety of crops, including wheat, barley, dates, olives, and grapes. This agricultural surplus not only sustained the local population but also became an essential commodity for trade.

Trade was a central pillar of Ebla's economy, and the city's merchants engaged in long-distance commerce with neighboring regions. Ebla's extensive trading networks reached as far as Egypt, Anatolia, Mesopotamia, and the Levant. Archaeological evidence, including the discovery of trade goods such as precious metals, pottery, and textiles from different regions, attests to the kingdom's robust commercial activities.

One of the most remarkable aspects of Ebla's rise was its administrative system, exemplified by the discovery of the Eblaite archives. These clay tablets, inscribed with cuneiform script, provide invaluable insights into the political, economic, and social aspects of Eblaite society. The archives, comprising thousands of tablets, document the kingdom's extensive diplomatic correspondence, trade agreements, and administrative records.

Ebla's diplomatic prowess played a crucial role in its rise as a regional power. The kingdom engaged in diplomatic exchanges with other city-states and kingdoms, forging alliances and establishing treaties. The Eblaite kings skillfully navigated the complex political landscape of the time, maintaining diplomatic relations with powerful neighboring entities such as Mari, Lagash, and Nagar. These diplomatic efforts allowed Ebla to expand its influence and protect its economic interests.

The Eblaite kings, through their diplomatic ties, also conducted marriage alliances, which further solidified their political position and fostered diplomatic stability. The marriage of Princess Gemdumash to the king of Mari and subsequent intermarriages with other ruling dynasties served to create alliances, secure trading partnerships, and establish mutual defense agreements.

Ebla's administrative and diplomatic capabilities were reflected in the city's urban planning and architectural achievements. The city featured a well-structured layout, with public buildings, temples, and palaces showcasing Eblaite craftsmanship and artistic expressions. The Royal Palace, with its grand halls and intricate wall paintings, stands as a testament to the kingdom's wealth and cultural sophistication.

Unfortunately, the rise of Ebla was followed by its eventual decline. Around 2250 BCE, the city was destroyed and abandoned, likely due to the conquest of the Akkadian Empire under Naram-Sin. The ruins of Ebla remained buried for centuries until their rediscovery in the 1970s.

The rise of Ebla and its achievements in trade and diplomacy left an enduring legacy. The kingdom's economic prosperity, diplomatic prowess, and administrative system set a precedent for subsequent civilizations in the region. The Eblaite archives, shedding light on the intricate details of ancient governance and international relations, provide a unique window into the political and economic dynamics of the time. The kingdom of Ebla serves as a testament to the complex tapestry of ancient Syrian history and its contributions to the development of early civilizations.

Kingdoms and Empires: From Mari to Ugarit

The era spanning from the late third millennium BCE to the late second millennium BCE witnessed the rise and fall of kingdoms and empires in the ancient land of Syria. During this period, notable civilizations such as Mari, Ebla, and Ugarit flourished, leaving a lasting impact on the region's history.

Mari, located along the Euphrates River, emerged as a powerful kingdom during the early second millennium BCE. The city's strategic location facilitated its rise as a major center for trade, diplomacy, and cultural exchange. Excavations at the site have unearthed a wealth of information about the Mariote kingdom, shedding light on its political structure, economic activities, and social customs.

The Mariote kingdom, under the rule of influential rulers like King Zimri-Lim, reached its pinnacle of power and prosperity. The kingdom's extensive archives, composed of thousands of cuneiform tablets, provide detailed insights into its administration, including legal codes, correspondence with foreign powers, and records of commercial transactions. The archives also reveal the kingdom's engagement in international diplomacy, as Mari maintained relationships with neighboring city-states and kingdoms.

Trade played a significant role in the economic success of Mari. The city became a hub for regional and long-distance commerce, fostering economic ties with regions as distant as Anatolia, Mesopotamia, and the Levant. The presence of diverse goods, including metals, textiles, and luxury items, in the archaeological record attests to the city's vibrant trading activities.

However, Mari's power and prosperity were short-lived. The kingdom eventually fell to the forces of the Babylonian Empire under Hammurabi in the early 18th century BCE, marking the end of Mari's independence and its absorption into the larger Mesopotamian political landscape.

Following the decline of Mari, other kingdoms rose to prominence in Syria. One of the most notable was Ebla, whose rise was discussed in the previous chapter. Ebla reached its peak during the mid-third millennium BCE, exhibiting extensive trade networks, administrative prowess, and diplomatic engagements. The kingdom's economic prosperity and cultural achievements left a profound impact on subsequent civilizations in the region.

Another significant kingdom of the time was Qatna, situated near modern-day Homs. Qatna emerged as a powerful city-state during the Middle Bronze Age and played a crucial role in regional politics and trade. The city's strategic location on major trade routes facilitated its economic growth, as it served as a transit point for goods traveling between Mesopotamia, Anatolia, and Egypt.

Qatna's archaeological remains provide evidence of its cultural and economic importance. The discovery of impressive palaces, temple structures, and royal tombs suggests a sophisticated society with a strong ruling elite. Artifacts found at Qatna, such as intricate ivory carvings and imported luxury items, highlight the city's participation in long-distance trade and its integration into the wider international network of the time.

Ugarit, located along the Mediterranean coast, emerged as a prominent city-state during the Late Bronze Age. Ugarit's rise can be attributed to its advantageous coastal position, facilitating maritime trade and cultural exchange with various civilizations of the time. The city's economic prosperity and cosmopolitan nature attracted merchants, diplomats, and artisans from Egypt, Anatolia, Cyprus, and other regions.

Ugarit's archives, discovered in the mid-20th century, provide invaluable insights into the political, economic, and cultural life of the city. The tablets, written in a unique cuneiform script called Ugaritic, offer a glimpse into Ugarit's administrative system, religious beliefs, literature, and international relations. The archives reveal the city's engagement in trade, diplomatic correspondence with other city-states, and its connections with major powers of the era, such as Egypt and the Hittite Empire. The downfall of Ugarit came with the upheavals of the Late Bronze Age collapse, a period of widespread unrest and migrations in the eastern Mediterranean region. The city was destroyed, likely due to invasions and conflicts, bringing an end to its prominence as a major cultural and commercial center.

The kingdoms and empires that rose and fell in ancient Syria during this period contributed to the vibrant tapestry of regional history. The political, economic, and cultural interactions among these civilizations laid the foundation for subsequent developments, leaving a legacy that continues to resonate in the archaeological record and the shared heritage of modern Syria.

The Hittite Influence on Syria

The Hittite Empire, centered in Anatolia (modern-day Turkey), exerted a significant influence on the region of Syria during the Late Bronze Age. The expansion of Hittite power brought about cultural, political, and economic interactions that left a lasting impact on Syria and its ancient civilizations.

The Hittites, an Indo-European people, began to establish their dominance in Anatolia around the 17th century BCE. Their gradual expansion southward brought them into contact with the city-states and kingdoms of northern Syria, leading to a fusion of Hittite and local cultures.

One notable aspect of the Hittite influence on Syria was the adoption of their ruling structure and administrative systems. The Hittites' well-organized bureaucracy and efficient governance played a crucial role in the administration of conquered territories, including parts of Syria. Hittite principles of governance, such as the appointment of local rulers and the integration of local elites into the empire's administrative apparatus, ensured a degree of continuity and stability in the region.

The Hittites' military campaigns and political alliances impacted the political landscape of Syria. The empire engaged in diplomatic relations and alliances with various city-states and kingdoms, including those in northern Syria. These alliances provided mutual benefits, as the Hittites secured military support and access to valuable resources, while the local rulers gained protection and favorable trade agreements.

One notable example of Hittite influence in Syria was the kingdom of Mitanni. The Mitanni rulers adopted Hittite military strategies, including the use of chariots and trained cavalry. This militaristic influence bolstered the power and influence of the Mitanni kingdom, enabling it to establish a formidable presence in the region.

Culturally, the Hittite influence can be seen in the artistic expressions and architectural styles of Syria. Hittite art, characterized by its distinctive hieroglyphic script and stylized representations of deities and mythological figures, found its way into Syrian art forms. This influence can be observed in the iconography and motifs depicted on sculptures, seals, and pottery unearthed from Syrian archaeological sites.

The Hittites' impact on trade and commerce was significant as well. The empire's control over key trade routes, particularly those connecting Anatolia with Syria and Mesopotamia, facilitated the flow of goods, ideas, and cultural practices. Hittite trade networks enhanced economic exchange between Syria and other regions, contributing to the prosperity and cultural diffusion in the ancient Near East.

Religiously, the Hittite pantheon and religious practices influenced the religious landscape of Syria. Local deities and cults in Syria often incorporated Hittite gods and rituals, resulting in syncretism and the development of hybrid religious traditions. The Hittite storm god, Teshub, for example, became assimilated into the local religious pantheon, sometimes equated with Syrian storm deities.

However, it is important to note that the Hittite presence in Syria was not limited to dominance and assimilation. The

Hittites also faced resistance from local populations and rival powers. Conflicts and power struggles arose as different factions vied for control over strategic territories and resources.

The decline of the Hittite Empire around the 12th century BCE led to a power vacuum in the region, and subsequent kingdoms and empires emerged to fill the void. Nevertheless, the Hittite influence on Syria left a profound imprint on the political, cultural, and religious landscape, shaping the course of history in the region.

The Hittite Empire's interactions with Syria showcased the dynamic nature of ancient civilizations and the cross-cultural exchanges that shaped their development. The fusion of Hittite and local cultures in Syria exemplifies the complexities of cultural assimilation and the interplay between conquerors and conquered. Understanding the Hittite influence on Syria contributes to our understanding of the diverse tapestry of ancient Near Eastern civilizations and their interconnectedness.

The Aramaeans: Nomads to Settlers

The Aramaeans, a Semitic-speaking people, played a significant role in the ancient history of Syria. Their migration and subsequent settlement in the region marked a transformative period characterized by cultural, linguistic, and political shifts.

Originating from the Arabian Peninsula, the Aramaeans were initially a nomadic people who traversed the vast expanses of the Near East. The exact timing of their migration into Syria is still a subject of scholarly debate, but it is generally believed to have occurred around the 12th century BCE.

The Aramaean migration into Syria was likely driven by a combination of factors, including population pressures, search for grazing lands for their herds, and opportunities for trade and economic advancement. As they entered the region, the Aramaeans encountered existing settled societies, such as the Hurrians, Amorites, and Hittites.

Initially, the Aramaeans maintained a semi-nomadic way of life, relying on pastoralism and small-scale agriculture. They lived in mobile tents and moved their herds seasonally to find suitable grazing areas. This mobile lifestyle allowed them to adapt to various ecological zones and establish trade networks across the region.

Over time, the Aramaeans began to transition from a purely nomadic existence to a more settled way of life. The allure of agricultural opportunities, the advantages of urban centers, and the influence of neighboring civilizations contributed to this transformation.

As they settled in different regions of Syria, the Aramaeans established numerous city-states, such as Damascus, Hamath, and Aleppo. These urban centers became hubs of economic activity, trade, and cultural exchange. The Aramaeans' integration into the regional political landscape led to the emergence of their kingdoms, which wielded varying degrees of power and influence.

The Aramaeans' transition from nomads to settlers also had linguistic implications. The Aramaic language, originally spoken by the Aramaean tribes, began to spread and develop into a lingua franca of the Near East. Aramaic gradually supplanted Akkadian, the dominant language of the region at the time, and became widely used for administration, commerce, and literary purposes.

The Aramaeans' cultural impact extended beyond language. They contributed to the cultural fusion and syncretism of the region, assimilating elements from other societies while retaining their distinct identity. Aramaean art, architecture, and religious practices reflected this cultural exchange, incorporating influences from neighboring civilizations.

Trade played a crucial role in the Aramaeans' settlement and integration into the regional network. The city-states established by the Aramaeans became important trade centers, facilitating the exchange of goods and ideas across vast distances. The strategic location of their cities along major trade routes, such as the Silk Road, enhanced their economic significance.

Politically, the Aramaean kingdoms developed their own dynasties and ruling elites. These kingdoms often had complex relationships with neighboring powers, such as the Neo-Assyrian Empire and the Neo-Babylonian Empire. The Aramaean kingdoms frequently interacted with these larger powers through diplomatic alliances, tribute payments, and occasional conflicts.

The Aramaean presence in Syria persisted for several centuries, but their political influence eventually waned with the rise of the Persian Empire. The Persian conquest of the region in the 6th century BCE brought about a new phase in Syrian history, with the Aramaeans gradually assimilating into the broader cultural and political framework of the empire.

The Aramaeans' transformation from nomads to settlers marked an important chapter in the history of Syria. Their settlement and cultural contributions played a vital role in shaping the regional landscape, laying the foundation for subsequent civilizations and the rich heritage of Syria. The Aramaeans' journey from nomadic tribes to urbanized societies exemplifies the adaptability and resilience of human civilizations in the face of changing circumstances.

Assyrian Dominance and Resistance

The period of Assyrian dominance and resistance in ancient Syria marks a significant chapter in the region's history. The rise of the Neo-Assyrian Empire, its campaigns of conquest, and the responses of local powers shaped the political, cultural, and military landscape of the time.

The Neo-Assyrian Empire emerged as a formidable power in the late 10th century BCE. Under rulers such as Ashurnasirpal II, Tiglath-Pileser III, and Sargon II, the empire expanded its territorial control, establishing dominance over vast stretches of the Near East, including parts of Syria.

Assyrian dominance was characterized by a combination of military might, strategic alliances, and administrative control. The empire's military campaigns aimed to assert authority, extract tribute, and maintain stability within its vast territories. These campaigns often brought Assyrian forces into direct contact with the local powers of Syria.

The Neo-Assyrians implemented a policy of imposing direct rule over conquered territories, including parts of Syria. They established provincial administrations, appointed governors, and introduced Assyrian administrative practices. This centralized control ensured loyalty, facilitated the collection of tribute, and maintained order within the empire.

Resistance to Assyrian dominance emerged among various factions in Syria. Local powers and city-states, such as Aram-Damascus, Israel, and Phoenician city-states, sought to assert their independence and resist Assyrian encroachment. They formed alliances, fortified their cities, and engaged in military campaigns to defend their autonomy.

One notable example of resistance was the coalition formed by the kings of Israel and Damascus against the Neo-Assyrians. This alliance, known as the Syro-Ephraimite coalition, aimed to counter Assyrian influence and maintain regional independence. However, the coalition's efforts ultimately proved unsuccessful, and both Israel and Damascus fell under Assyrian control.

The Neo-Assyrian Empire employed a strategy of terror and intimidation to maintain control over its territories. The empire's reputation for ruthless military tactics, including mass deportations, forced resettlements, and the destruction of rebellious cities, instilled fear among potential resistors. This approach aimed to deter further challenges to Assyrian authority.

Despite Assyrian dominance, pockets of resistance persisted in Syria. Local leaders, fortified cities, and guerrilla warfare tactics allowed some regions to resist assimilation into the Assyrian administration. The Aramaean kingdom of Bit-Bahiani, for example, successfully maintained its independence for an extended period, engaging in intermittent conflicts with the Assyrians.

Assyrian dominance in Syria also had cultural and artistic implications. The empire's influence on the region's cultural practices, architecture, and art can be seen in the adoption of Assyrian motifs, stylistic elements, and architectural techniques. This cultural assimilation was a result of both direct influence and the aspiration of local powers to align themselves with the dominant empire.

The decline of the Neo-Assyrian Empire in the late 7th century BCE led to a shift in the power dynamics of the region. The rise of the Neo-Babylonian Empire, along with the aspirations of regional powers like the Medes and the Persians, challenged Assyrian dominance. These forces ultimately toppled the Assyrian empire and reconfigured the political landscape of Syria and the wider Near East.

The period of Assyrian dominance and resistance highlights the complex dynamics of power, conquest, and resilience in ancient Syria. The Neo-Assyrian Empire's military prowess and administrative control left a profound impact on the region, while the resistance efforts of local powers demonstrated their determination to safeguard their autonomy. Understanding this era enriches our comprehension of the intricate web of political and cultural interactions that shaped the history of ancient Syria.

The Neo-Babylonian and Persian Rule

The period of Neo-Babylonian and Persian rule in ancient Syria marks a significant chapter in the region's history. The rise of the Neo-Babylonian Empire, followed by the ascendancy of the Persian Achaemenid Empire, brought about profound political, cultural, and economic changes.

The Neo-Babylonian Empire, also known as the Chaldean Empire, emerged as a dominant power in the late 7th century BCE. Under the leadership of King Nabopolassar and his son Nebuchadnezzar II, the empire expanded its control over vast territories, including parts of Syria.

The Neo-Babylonian rule over Syria was characterized by a combination of military campaigns, diplomacy, and administrative control. Nebuchadnezzar II conducted several successful military expeditions into the Levant, including campaigns against the kingdom of Judah and the Phoenician city-states. These conquests brought parts of Syria, including cities like Damascus and Tyre, under Babylonian control.

The Neo-Babylonians established a system of provincial administration to govern their territories, including those in Syria. Local rulers were often allowed to retain their positions, but under the overall authority of the Babylonian empire. This administrative approach aimed to maintain stability, extract tribute, and integrate conquered territories into the empire's economic and political structure.

The Babylonian rule in Syria had cultural and artistic implications. The influence of Babylonian culture can be seen in the adoption of Babylonian architectural styles, religious practices, and artistic motifs in Syrian cities. The Babylonians also contributed to the development of astronomical knowledge, mathematical systems, and literature, which had a lasting impact on the intellectual heritage of the region.

The decline of the Neo-Babylonian Empire came with the rise of the Persian Achaemenid Empire. Led by Cyrus the Great, the Persians overthrew the Babylonian empire and established their rule over Syria and other territories in the mid-6th century BCE.

The Persian rule in Syria brought about a period of political stability and administrative reorganization. The Achaemenid Empire implemented a decentralized system of governance, known as the satrapy system, which allowed a degree of regional autonomy while maintaining Persian control. Satraps, appointed by the Persian king, governed the provinces and ensured the collection of tribute.

Under Persian rule, Syria experienced economic growth and cultural exchange. The empire's extensive road network facilitated trade and commerce, connecting Syria with other regions of the empire. The Persian influence on trade routes and economic policies contributed to the prosperity and development of urban centers in Syria, such as Damascus and Palmyra.

Culturally, the Persian period saw a fusion of Persian and local traditions. Persian religious practices, such as Zoroastrianism, coexisted with the existing religious beliefs of the region. Persian artistic styles and motifs also influenced the architecture, sculpture, and decorative arts of Syria.

The Persian Empire's rule in Syria faced occasional challenges and rebellions. Local powers and regional kingdoms, such as the Phoenicians and the Medes, aspired to assert their independence and resist Persian control. However, the Persian Empire maintained a strong grip on Syria for several centuries.

The decline of the Persian Empire came with the conquests of Alexander the Great in the 4th century BCE, bringing an end to Persian rule in the region. Alexander's conquests initiated a new phase in Syrian history, blending Hellenistic influences with existing cultural and political traditions.

The Neo-Babylonian and Persian rule in Syria played a vital role in shaping the region's history and heritage. The empires' administrative structures, cultural exchanges, and economic policies left indelible imprints on the cities, art forms, and societal dynamics of ancient Syria. Understanding this era provides insights into the interplay of power, cultural assimilation, and the enduring legacies of ancient civilizations in Syria.

Alexander the Great and Hellenistic Syria

The arrival of Alexander the Great in Syria marked a transformative period in the region's history. The conquests of Alexander and the subsequent Hellenistic era brought about significant political, cultural, and social changes to ancient Syria.

Alexander the Great, the Macedonian king, embarked on a series of military campaigns in the 4th century BCE, aiming to conquer the Persian Empire and expand his own empire. In 333 BCE, Alexander invaded the Achaemenid territories, which included Syria.

The conquest of Syria by Alexander the Great was a swift and decisive campaign. Cities and territories in Syria, including Damascus and Tyre, fell to Alexander's forces. The Persians, who had ruled the region, were ousted, and the Macedonians established their dominance.

Alexander's rule in Syria marked the beginning of the Hellenistic period. The term "Hellenistic" refers to the spread of Greek culture, language, and political systems across the conquered territories. The influence of Greek civilization, known as Hellenism, had a profound impact on the region.

Under Hellenistic rule, the Greek language became widely spoken, and Greek administrative systems were implemented. Greek cities, known as polis, were established throughout Syria, including cities like Antioch,

Seleucia Pieria, and Apamea. These cities served as centers of Greek culture, administration, and trade.

The Hellenistic era in Syria witnessed a fusion of Greek and local traditions. While Greek customs and institutions took root, local cultural practices and beliefs also persisted. This cultural syncretism resulted in a vibrant and diverse society that blended Greek, Persian, Egyptian, and Mesopotamian influences.

One of the most notable aspects of Hellenistic Syria was the founding of the Seleucid Empire. Following Alexander's death in 323 BCE, his generals vied for control over his empire. Seleucus I Nicator emerged as the ruler of the Seleucid Empire, which encompassed much of Alexander's former territories, including Syria.

The Seleucid Empire played a significant role in the political, economic, and cultural development of Syria. The empire's capital, Antioch, became a cosmopolitan center and a hub of Hellenistic civilization. It attracted scholars, philosophers, and artists, fostering intellectual and cultural exchange.

The Seleucid rulers pursued a policy of cultural assimilation, encouraging the spread of Greek language, education, and customs. They established Greek-style institutions, such as gymnasiums and theaters, which became integral to the urban landscape of Syrian cities.

However, the Seleucid Empire faced challenges and conflicts throughout its existence. Local powers and rival kingdoms, such as the Ptolemaic Kingdom in Egypt, the Parthians in Persia, and various native rebellions, posed threats to Seleucid control. The empire experienced periods of territorial losses and internal struggles, leading to its gradual decline.

Despite the challenges, Hellenistic influence endured in Syria even after the decline of the Seleucid Empire. Greek cultural and artistic expressions continued to flourish, leaving a lasting impact on architecture, sculpture, and literature. The works of renowned Hellenistic poets and philosophers, such as Theocritus and Epicurus, influenced the intellectual and literary circles of Syria.

The Hellenistic era in Syria also witnessed the blending of Greek and local religious practices. Greek gods and goddesses were assimilated into the local pantheon, and religious syncretism became common. Local deities continued to be worshipped alongside the Greek gods, reflecting the complex religious landscape of Hellenistic Syria.

The Hellenistic period in Syria eventually gave way to the rise of the Roman Empire in the 1st century BCE. The Romans gradually asserted their dominance over the region, incorporating it into their vast empire. Roman rule brought new political, cultural, and architectural influences to Syria, shaping its future trajectory.

The era of Alexander the Great and Hellenistic Syria stands as a pivotal moment in the region's history. The spread of Greek culture and the establishment of Greek-influenced cities transformed the societal fabric of Syria. The cultural syncretism and intellectual exchanges that occurred during this period laid the groundwork for the diverse heritage of the region.

The Seleucid Dynasty: Greek and Persian Fusion

The Seleucid Dynasty, which emerged in the wake of Alexander the Great's conquests, brought together Greek and Persian influences in a fusion that shaped the cultural, political, and social landscape of the ancient Near East. The Seleucid Empire, under the rule of the Seleucid kings, encompassed vast territories, including present-day Syria, Iran, and parts of Central Asia.

Seleucus I Nicator, one of Alexander's generals, established the Seleucid Empire in the early 4th century BCE. The empire inherited a diverse range of cultural traditions, with Greek and Persian elements being the most prominent. The Seleucid rulers embraced this fusion and sought to consolidate their rule by incorporating and reconciling Greek and Persian customs.

One of the notable aspects of Seleucid rule was the adoption of Greek administrative systems and institutions. Greek cities, known as polis, were founded across the empire, including cities like Antioch, Seleucia, and Laodicea. These cities became centers of Hellenistic culture, housing Greek-style agora (marketplaces), theaters, and gymnasiums. Greek language, education, and philosophy became prominent, creating a sense of Greek cultural identity within the empire.

At the same time, the Seleucids recognized the importance of incorporating Persian influences to maintain stability and secure the loyalty of their subjects. They retained elements of the Achaemenid administrative structure, including the division of the empire into satrapies and the appointment of local officials. Persian nobility and aristocracy were often integrated into the Seleucid court and administration, fostering a sense of continuity with the pre-existing Persian traditions.

Cultural and religious syncretism was a hallmark of the Seleucid Empire. Greek deities, such as Zeus and Apollo, were worshipped alongside Persian and local gods. The Seleucid kings, while presenting themselves as successors to Alexander's legacy, also adopted Persian titles and participated in traditional Persian religious rituals. This blending of religious practices reflected the empire's multicultural nature and the rulers' desire to maintain the allegiance of diverse populations.

The Seleucid Empire facilitated cultural exchanges and intellectual flourishing. Greek scholars, philosophers, and artists were drawn to the vibrant centers of the empire, contributing to a rich cultural milieu. The Library of Antioch, a renowned center of learning, attracted scholars from various disciplines and helped disseminate Greek knowledge throughout the empire.

Art and architecture also showcased the fusion of Greek and Persian styles. Greek architectural elements, such as columned temples and monumental sculptures, blended with Persian influences, such as the use of decorative motifs, intricate reliefs, and the incorporation of Persian architectural features like the iwan. This fusion resulted in unique architectural forms and artistic expressions, exemplified by the palaces, tombs, and monuments of the Seleucid era.

The Seleucid Empire faced challenges and conflicts throughout its existence. Regional powers, such as the Ptolemaic Kingdom in Egypt and the Parthians in Persia, vied for control over territories within the empire. Internal power struggles, revolts, and pressures from nomadic groups also posed threats to Seleucid authority.

The decline of the Seleucid Empire came gradually, as internal strife and external pressures weakened its hold over the vast territories. In the 2nd century BCE, the empire began to fragment, with regional powers asserting their independence and establishing their own kingdoms.

The Seleucid Dynasty left a lasting impact on the region. The fusion of Greek and Persian cultures facilitated the transmission of Greek thought and knowledge to the East, while also preserving elements of the Persian heritage. The empire's administrative structures, cultural exchanges, and artistic developments shaped the future trajectory of the region, contributing to its rich and diverse historical legacy.

Palmyra: Queen of the Syrian Desert

Palmyra, also known as Tadmor in ancient times, holds a unique place in the history of Syria as a remarkable city situated in the heart of the Syrian Desert. This chapter explores the rise, splendor, and significance of Palmyra as a flourishing center of commerce, culture, and crossroads of civilizations.

The origins of Palmyra can be traced back to the 2nd millennium BCE when it served as a small oasis settlement in the arid desert landscape. Its strategic location along the caravan routes connecting the Mediterranean with the East made it a vital hub for trade, linking Mesopotamia, Persia, India, and the Arabian Peninsula.

Palmyra's rise to prominence occurred during the 1st century BCE when it became an independent city-state under Arab rule. The city's strategic positioning and its ability to control and protect the lucrative trade routes allowed it to prosper and grow in wealth and influence.

Under the leadership of Queen Zenobia in the 3rd century CE, Palmyra experienced its golden age. Zenobia, a skilled and ambitious ruler, expanded Palmyra's territory, establishing a short-lived Palmyrene Empire that encompassed parts of Syria, Egypt, and Anatolia. Her rule brought Palmyra to the height of its power and prestige, challenging the authority of the Roman Empire.

Palmyra's architectural marvels were a testament to its grandeur and wealth. The city boasted impressive structures, including temples, colonnaded streets, tombs, and public buildings. The Great Colonnade, a mile-long avenue lined with towering columns, exemplified the city's architectural prowess and served as a symbol of its prosperity.

The Temple of Bel, dedicated to the ancient Semitic god Bel, stood as one of the most important religious structures in Palmyra. Its grandeur, with intricately carved reliefs and towering columns, attested to the city's religious devotion and cultural significance. The Temple of Baalshamin, the Temple of Nabu, and the Temple of Allat were among the other notable religious sites that enriched the city's architectural landscape.

Palmyra's cultural heritage was characterized by a unique blend of Eastern and Western influences. Its location at the crossroads of civilizations facilitated cultural exchange, resulting in a distinct Palmyrene art style that incorporated elements from Greek, Roman, Persian, and local traditions. Sculptures, reliefs, and funerary art showcased a fusion of styles and reflected the multicultural nature of the city.

The people of Palmyra, known as Palmyrenes, were a diverse mix of ethnic groups, including Arabs, Greeks, Romans, and Persians. This diversity contributed to the cosmopolitan nature of the city, fostering a rich cultural tapestry and vibrant intellectual life. Palmyrenes were known for their linguistic abilities, with Aramaic serving as the primary language, but Greek and Latin also being widely spoken.

Trade was the lifeblood of Palmyra's economy. Caravans laden with goods, including spices, silk, precious metals, and exotic merchandise, traversed the desert routes, making Palmyra a thriving center of commerce. The city's merchants and traders amassed considerable wealth and played a significant role in the wider trade networks of the ancient world.

Palmyra's decline came with the resurgence of the Roman Empire and its reconquest of the city in the 3rd century CE. The Romans, fearing the growing power of Palmyra under Zenobia's rule, reasserted their authority, quelling the Palmyrene rebellion and incorporating the city back into the Roman domain.

Tragically, the ancient city of Palmyra fell victim to the destructive forces of human conflict in recent years. Its architectural treasures and historical sites suffered extensive damage during the Syrian civil war, resulting in an irreparable loss to world heritage.

Despite the destruction, Palmyra's legacy endures. Its cultural and historical significance as a symbol of resilience, multiculturalism, and architectural excellence continues to captivate scholars and enthusiasts worldwide. Efforts to preserve and reconstruct the city's heritage serve as a reminder of Palmyra's enduring impact on the history and cultural mosaic of Syria and the wider ancient world.

The Roman Conquest and Pax Romana

The Roman conquest and the subsequent establishment of Pax Romana, or Roman peace, brought profound changes to the region of Syria. This chapter delves into the period of Roman rule, highlighting the conquest, administration, and the transformative influence of Roman culture on Syria.

The Roman conquest of Syria began in the 1st century BCE and unfolded gradually over several decades. Syria, with its strategic location and rich resources, attracted the attention of the expanding Roman Republic. In 64 BCE, the Roman general Pompey the Great conquered the region, incorporating it into the Roman Republic.

Roman rule in Syria introduced a new administrative framework. The region was organized as a province within the Roman Empire, overseen by a governor appointed by the Roman Senate. The Roman administration brought stability, effective governance, and the enforcement of Roman law, establishing a system that would endure for centuries.

One significant aspect of Roman rule was the construction of infrastructure, including roads, aqueducts, and public buildings. The Romans built an extensive network of roads that connected Syria with other parts of the empire, facilitating trade, communication, and the movement of troops. Aqueducts brought water to urban centers, improving sanitation and the quality of life.

The Roman presence in Syria also brought about urban development and architectural advancements. Cities, such as Antioch, Damascus, and Palmyra, experienced significant growth and became flourishing centers of trade, culture, and governance. Roman architectural styles influenced the construction of public buildings, temples, theaters, and other monumental structures, leaving an indelible mark on the urban landscape.

Roman culture and language permeated Syrian society. Latin became the administrative language, while Greek, the lingua franca of the eastern Mediterranean, continued to be widely spoken. The spread of Roman customs, dress, and social norms contributed to the Romanization of Syrian society, although local traditions and languages persisted among the diverse population.

Religiously, the Romans embraced a policy of religious tolerance, allowing the diverse religious practices of the region to continue. The Roman pantheon of gods was introduced alongside local deities, enabling the coexistence and syncretism of various religious beliefs. Cults dedicated to Roman gods, such as Jupiter and Venus, found followers among the Syrian population.

Trade and commerce flourished under Roman rule. Syria's position as a crossroads of civilizations and its proximity to important trade routes facilitated economic growth. Agricultural products, textiles, spices, and luxury goods from Syria found eager markets within the empire, contributing to the region's prosperity.

The establishment of Pax Romana brought a period of relative peace and stability to Syria. The Roman Empire's military might ensured the suppression of rebellions and the enforcement of Roman authority. This peace allowed for the flourishing of cultural and intellectual pursuits, the promotion of trade, and the integration of Syria into the broader Roman world.

Pax Romana also facilitated the spread of ideas, intellectual exchange, and the dissemination of Roman culture. Syrian cities became centers of learning and attracted scholars, philosophers, and artists. The renowned School of Antioch, for instance, produced notable figures like Lucian of Samosata and John Chrysostom, who made significant contributions to literature, philosophy, and theology.

However, the Roman period in Syria was not without challenges. The region faced periodic revolts and conflicts, particularly during times of political upheaval within the wider empire. Local uprisings and power struggles among regional powers, such as the Jewish revolts, challenged Roman control but were eventually subdued.

The decline of the Roman Empire in the 4th century CE brought about a new phase in Syrian history. The region experienced invasions by various external forces, including the Sassanian Persians and the Arab Muslims, leading to the end of Roman rule and the subsequent transformation of the region.

The Roman conquest and Pax Romana left an enduring impact on Syria. Romanization influenced the region's language, culture, architecture, and governance. The legacy of Roman rule in Syria, evident in its archaeological sites and cultural heritage, continues to shape our understanding of the region's rich and complex history.

Christianity Takes Root in Syria

The spread and establishment of Christianity in Syria marked a significant chapter in the history of the region. This chapter explores the origins, growth, and influence of Christianity in Syria, highlighting its cultural, religious, and societal impact.

Christianity's roots in Syria can be traced back to the life and teachings of Jesus Christ in the 1st century CE. It was in this region, particularly in the city of Antioch, that the followers of Jesus first began to be called "Christians." Antioch emerged as an important center for early Christian communities, playing a pivotal role in the spread of the faith.

The conversion of the apostle Paul, a prominent figure in early Christianity, on the road to Damascus in Syria is a significant event in the history of the religion. Paul's conversion experience and subsequent missionary efforts contributed to the rapid dissemination of Christian beliefs in Syria and beyond.

Syria's cultural diversity and its strategic location as a crossroads of civilizations facilitated the spread of Christianity. The region was home to various ethnic and religious groups, including Jews, Greeks, Romans, and Arameans. The message of Christianity resonated with different communities, attracting followers from diverse backgrounds.

The cities of Antioch, Damascus, and Edessa (now Urfa) emerged as important Christian centers in Syria. Antioch, in particular, played a crucial role in the early development of Christian theology and the formation of the Antiochene School, known for its emphasis on biblical interpretation and the proclamation of the Gospel.

Christianity's influence extended beyond religious beliefs. The establishment of Christian communities led to the formation of early Christian institutions, including churches, monasteries, and schools. The Monastery of Saint Simeon Stylites, located near Aleppo, is a notable example of an early Christian monastery in Syria that attracted pilgrims and played a significant role in the spiritual life of the region.

Syria's status as an important intellectual and cultural center during the Byzantine era further contributed to the growth of Christianity. The translation of biblical texts, the development of theological doctrines, and the engagement in debates and discussions shaped the intellectual landscape of Syrian Christianity.

Syrian theologians and scholars made significant contributions to the development of Christian thought. Figures like John Chrysostom, a renowned preacher and theologian from Antioch, and Ephrem the Syrian, a poet and hymnographer, left a lasting impact on Christian theology and spirituality.

The emergence of distinct Christian traditions and the establishment of various sects further enriched the religious landscape of Syria. Syrian Christianity encompassed different groups, including the Syriac Orthodox Church, the Melkite Greek Catholic Church, the Maronite Church, and the Assyrian Church of the East. These traditions preserved unique liturgical practices, theological perspectives, and cultural expressions.

Syria's Christian communities faced periods of persecution and challenges throughout history. Roman authorities and subsequent rulers, including Byzantine emperors and later Islamic caliphates, imposed restrictions and occasionally persecuted Christians. However, Christian communities persevered, adapting to changing circumstances and preserving their faith and traditions.

The advent of Islam in the 7th century CE brought a new religious and political landscape to Syria. The rise of Islamic empires led to the transformation of the region and the coexistence of Christians and Muslims. Over the centuries, Christians in Syria continued to contribute to the region's cultural, intellectual, and religious heritage.

Today, Christianity remains an integral part of the Syrian social fabric, albeit with a diminished presence due to various historical factors and contemporary challenges. The Christian communities in Syria, with their rich history and cultural contributions, bear witness to the enduring legacy of Christianity's roots in the region.

The story of Christianity taking root in Syria is a testament to the resilience of faith and the intricate interplay between religion, culture, and history. Understanding the history of Christianity in Syria provides valuable insights into the diverse tapestry of religious traditions that have shaped the region and its people.

Byzantine Syria: Center of Christian Civilization

The Byzantine era in Syria, spanning from the 4th to the 7th century CE, was a period of significant religious, cultural, and architectural development. This chapter explores Byzantine Syria as a center of Christian civilization, highlighting its religious institutions, artistic achievements, and the enduring legacy of Byzantine influence.

Under Byzantine rule, Christianity became the official religion of the empire, and the Byzantine Emperors actively supported and promoted Christian institutions and practices. Syria, with its strong Christian communities and historical significance, emerged as a vital center for the spread and preservation of Christian civilization.

The Byzantine era witnessed the construction of numerous churches and monasteries throughout Syria. Prominent among them was the Church of Saint Simeon Stylites, a monumental structure near Aleppo dedicated to the ascetic Saint Simeon. This church, along with many others, exemplified the Byzantine architectural style, characterized by elaborate mosaics, intricate carvings, and a sense of grandeur.

Damascus, the capital of Syria during the Byzantine era, became an important Christian center. The city housed notable churches such as the Cathedral of Saint John the Baptist, known for its splendid mosaics, and the Church of Saint Paul. These churches served as places of worship, pilgrimage, and theological discourse, fostering a vibrant religious and intellectual atmosphere.

Monasticism played a significant role in Byzantine Syria, with the establishment of monastic communities and the rise of influential monastic figures. Monasteries, such as the Monastery of Saint Moses the Abyssinian near Homs and the Monastery of Saint Maron in the mountains of Lebanon, offered havens for prayer, study, and spiritual contemplation.

The theological and intellectual heritage of Byzantine Christianity thrived in Syrian cities, attracting renowned theologians, scholars, and philosophers. Figures like John of Damascus, known for his theological treatises and defense of Christian beliefs, contributed to the intellectual richness of Byzantine Syria.

Art and iconography flourished during the Byzantine era, leaving a lasting impact on the artistic traditions of Syria. Icon painting, characterized by its stylized representations of religious figures, became a prominent form of artistic expression. Byzantine icons, with their spiritual and symbolic significance, adorned churches, monasteries, and private homes.

The influence of Byzantine Syria extended beyond religious and artistic realms. The region played a crucial role in trade, connecting the Mediterranean world with the Arabian Peninsula, Persia, and beyond. Syrian cities, such as Antioch, Aleppo, and Damascus, were vibrant commercial centers, bustling with economic activity and cultural exchange.

The Byzantine period also witnessed the emergence of prominent Syrian Christian communities, including the Greek Orthodox, Syriac Orthodox, and Melkite Greek Catholic churches. These communities preserved their distinct liturgical traditions, theological perspectives, and cultural practices, contributing to the diverse religious landscape of Byzantine Syria.

Despite its cultural and religious achievements, Byzantine Syria faced challenges and disruptions. The rise of Islamic caliphates in the 7th century CE led to the gradual decline of Byzantine authority and the introduction of a new political and religious order in the region.

The legacy of Byzantine Syria endures through its architectural marvels, artistic treasures, and the intellectual and spiritual contributions of its theologians and thinkers. The mosaics, frescoes, and ancient ruins scattered across the Syrian landscape serve as reminders of the vibrant Christian civilization that once thrived in the region.

Today, the remnants of Byzantine Syria stand as a testament to the enduring influence of Christianity and its role in shaping the cultural and historical heritage of the region. The Byzantine era remains a significant chapter in Syria's past, illustrating the interconnectedness of religion, art, and civilization.

The Muslim Conquest: Damascus and the Umayyads

The Muslim conquest of Syria in the 7th century CE marked a turning point in the region's history, ushering in a new era of Islamic rule and the rise of the Umayyad Caliphate. This chapter explores the events surrounding the Muslim conquest, the significance of Damascus as the capital of the caliphate, and the enduring legacy of the Umayyad dynasty.

In the early 7th century CE, the Arabian Peninsula witnessed the emergence of Islam and the teachings of the Prophet Muhammad. Islam spread rapidly, uniting Arab tribes and creating a powerful force. Under the leadership of the caliphs, successors to Muhammad, the Arab Muslims embarked on a series of conquests to expand the Islamic empire.

The Muslim conquest of Syria began in 634 CE, with the Rashidun Caliphate under the command of Khalid ibn al-Walid. The Arab armies advanced swiftly, capturing key cities and engaging in battles with Byzantine forces. The capture of Damascus in 635 CE proved to be a significant turning point, as the city became the capital of the newly established Islamic administration in the region.

Damascus, with its strategic location and rich history, held both political and cultural significance. The city had a well-developed infrastructure, including an extensive water system and architectural marvels from previous civilizations. The Umayyad Caliphs recognized the importance of Damascus and made it their center of power and governance.

Under the Umayyad Caliphate, Damascus experienced a period of growth and prosperity. The city's economy flourished, benefiting from the extensive trade networks that connected the Islamic empire with the Mediterranean world, Africa, and Asia. Wealth poured into Damascus, transforming it into a cosmopolitan hub of commerce and cultural exchange.

The Umayyad Caliphs left an indelible mark on Damascus through architectural achievements. The most notable example is the Umayyad Mosque, also known as the Great Mosque of Damascus. Built during the reign of Caliph Al-Walid I, the mosque stands as a testament to the architectural prowess of the Umayyads. Its grandeur, adorned with intricate mosaics, stunning minarets, and a monumental prayer hall, exemplifies the fusion of Islamic and Byzantine architectural styles.

The Umayyad dynasty played a significant role in shaping the religious, cultural, and political landscape of Syria. They promoted Arabic as the language of administration and governance, leading to the widespread adoption of the Arabic language throughout the region. The Umayyads also consolidated Islamic law and established administrative structures, laying the foundation for the spread and institutionalization of Islam.

Despite the centralization of power in Damascus, the Umayyad Caliphs faced challenges and opposition. Discontent among various segments of society, regional tensions, and internal power struggles occasionally threatened the stability of the caliphate. The Umayyads also faced opposition from the emerging Abbasid dynasty, who eventually overthrew and replaced them in 750 CE.

The Umayyad dynasty left a lasting impact on Syria and the wider Islamic world. Their patronage of arts, architecture, and literature resulted in a vibrant cultural scene. Umayyad artistic traditions, such as the use of intricate calligraphy and geometric patterns, influenced Islamic art and architecture for centuries to come.

The decline of the Umayyad Caliphate in Syria led to the fragmentation of political authority in the region. Various regional powers, including local dynasties and provincial governors, established their own rule over different parts of Syria. This period witnessed the rise of powerful emirates, such as the Hamdanids, the Fatimids, and the Seljuks, who shaped the political landscape of Syria in the following centuries.

The Muslim conquest and the Umayyad rule in Syria transformed the religious, cultural, and political fabric of the region. Islam became the dominant religion, and Arabic became the primary language of communication. The architectural and artistic achievements of the Umayyads, particularly in Damascus, left a profound impact on the region's heritage.

Today, the Umayyad Mosque stands as a symbol of Damascus's historical and cultural significance, attracting visitors from around the world. The legacy of the Umayyads and the Muslim conquest continues to shape Syria's identity, reminding us of the rich and complex history of the region and its role in the development of Islamic civilization.

The Abbasid Era: Intellectual and Cultural Flourishing

The Abbasid era, spanning from the 8th to the 13th century CE, marked a significant period of intellectual and cultural flourishing in the Islamic world. This chapter explores the achievements and contributions of the Abbasid dynasty, highlighting their patronage of scholarship, scientific advancements, and the preservation and transmission of knowledge.

The Abbasid dynasty emerged as the ruling power in the Islamic empire after overthrowing the Umayyad Caliphate in 750 CE. The Abbasids established their capital in Baghdad, which soon became a vibrant center of learning, attracting scholars, scientists, and philosophers from far and wide.

Under Abbasid rule, Baghdad became a beacon of intellectual and cultural exchange. The House of Wisdom (Bayt al-Hikmah), founded by Caliph al-Ma'mun, served as a renowned institution for translating and preserving Greek, Persian, and other ancient texts. Scholars from diverse backgrounds worked tirelessly to translate and study these texts, contributing to the preservation and transmission of knowledge from classical civilizations.

The Abbasid era witnessed a flourishing of Islamic philosophy, literature, and the arts. Prominent figures like Al-Kindi, Al-Farabi, and Ibn Sina (Avicenna) made significant contributions to various fields, including philosophy, mathematics, medicine, and astronomy. Their works, written in Arabic, synthesized and expanded upon the knowledge of earlier civilizations, becoming influential not only within the Islamic world but also in Europe during the Middle Ages.

One of the enduring legacies of the Abbasid era was the advancement of mathematics and science. Scholars such as Al-Khwarizmi, known as the "Father of Algebra," made significant contributions to the field of mathematics, introducing concepts like algebra and algorithms. The study of astronomy flourished, with the construction of observatories and the development of sophisticated instruments for celestial observations.

The translation movement sponsored by the Abbasids facilitated the translation of Greek, Persian, and Indian works into Arabic. This intellectual exchange led to the assimilation of diverse knowledge, fostering an environment of cross-cultural learning. Islamic scholars not only preserved ancient wisdom but also built upon it, synthesizing it with their own insights and expanding the frontiers of knowledge.

The patronage of arts and literature by the Abbasid rulers contributed to a rich cultural tapestry. Arabic poetry, known for its lyrical beauty and intricacy, flourished during this period. Literary works, such as the Thousand and One Nights, captivated audiences with their imaginative storytelling. Architecture also reached new heights, with the construction of grand mosques, palaces, and public buildings, showcasing exquisite craftsmanship and geometric designs.

The Abbasid era also witnessed religious and sectarian developments within Islam. The spread of Shia Islam, particularly the emergence of the Fatimid dynasty in North

Africa and the rise of other Shia dynasties, presented a challenge to Abbasid authority. Theological debates and rivalries between different Islamic sects and schools of thought added complexity to the religious landscape of the time.

The Abbasid Caliphate faced political challenges, including regional revolts, territorial fragmentation, and external pressures from neighboring powers. The decline of centralized Abbasid authority led to the rise of local dynasties and regional powers that exerted their own influence in various parts of the empire.

Despite these challenges, the Abbasid era left an enduring legacy of intellectual, cultural, and scientific achievements. The translation movement, the advancement of knowledge in various disciplines, and the promotion of arts and literature contributed to a golden age of Islamic civilization. The intellectual achievements of this era laid the groundwork for the European Renaissance, as Arabic texts were translated into Latin and disseminated throughout Europe.

The Abbasid era stands as a testament to the power of knowledge, the pursuit of wisdom, and the cross-cultural exchange that characterized the Islamic world during this period. The intellectual and cultural achievements of the Abbasid dynasty continue to inspire and shape our understanding of the diverse and rich history of the Islamic civilization.

The Crusaders and the Kingdom of Jerusalem

The Crusaders' arrival in the Levant in the 11th century CE marked a significant chapter in the history of Syria, particularly in the establishment of the Kingdom of Jerusalem. This chapter explores the motivations behind the Crusades, the events surrounding the creation of the Kingdom of Jerusalem, and the impact of Crusader rule on the region.

The Crusades were a series of military campaigns launched by Western European Christians in response to a call for aid from the Byzantine Empire and the perceived threat to Christian holy sites in the Holy Land. The First Crusade, which began in 1096 CE, resulted in the capture of Jerusalem by the Crusader forces in 1099 CE.

Following the capture of Jerusalem, the Crusaders established the Kingdom of Jerusalem, one of several Crusader states that emerged in the region. The Kingdom of Jerusalem encompassed parts of present-day Israel, Palestine, and Jordan, and it became a feudal state ruled by Crusader nobility.

The Crusader rulers sought to establish a Christian kingdom in the Levant, with Jerusalem as its spiritual and political center. They implemented a feudal system and established a hierarchy of nobles, clergy, and commoners within the kingdom. The Latin Patriarchate of Jerusalem served as the ecclesiastical authority, overseeing the religious affairs of the Crusader territories.

Crusader rule in the Kingdom of Jerusalem was marked by a fusion of Western European and local traditions. The Crusaders adopted elements of the local culture and incorporated them into their own practices. This blending of cultures influenced various aspects of life, including architecture, language, and social customs.

The Crusader period witnessed the construction of numerous fortresses, castles, and churches throughout the kingdom. The most iconic example is the Church of the Holy Sepulchre in Jerusalem, believed to be the site of Jesus' crucifixion and burial. These structures exhibited a mix of architectural styles, incorporating both Western European and Byzantine influences.

The Kingdom of Jerusalem faced constant challenges from both Muslim forces and internal divisions among the Crusader nobility. Muslim rulers, including Saladin, launched counter-offensives to reclaim the captured territories, leading to a series of conflicts known as the Crusader-Muslim Wars. These conflicts culminated in the loss of Jerusalem to Saladin's forces in 1187 CE.

Despite the challenges, the Crusader period left a lasting impact on the region. The presence of Crusader states led to increased contact and cultural exchange between the Christian West and the Muslim East. The Crusaders introduced new agricultural techniques, such as the cultivation of sugar cane, and facilitated trade routes between Europe and the Levant.

The Crusades also brought about religious fervor and pilgrimage to the Holy Land. Pilgrims from Western Europe traveled to Jerusalem and other Christian holy sites, contributing to the economic and cultural vitality of the region. The influence of the Crusaders extended beyond the military and political sphere, leaving traces in literature, art, and legends.

Over time, the Crusader states faced gradual decline and were eventually conquered by Muslim forces. The fall of Acre, the last major Crusader stronghold, in 1291 CE marked the end of Crusader presence in the Levant. The legacy of the Crusader period, however, continued to shape perceptions and memories of the Holy Land in the centuries that followed.

The Crusaders' rule in the Kingdom of Jerusalem remains a complex and contested period in the history of the region. It is viewed differently by different communities and is often a topic of historical debate and analysis. Today, the Crusader castles and archaeological remains stand as reminders of this medieval chapter, offering glimpses into the interplay of cultures and the shifting political dynamics of the time.

The Ayyubids: Salahuddin and the Reconquest

The Ayyubids, a prominent Muslim dynasty, played a pivotal role in the history of Syria during the 12th and 13th centuries CE. This chapter explores the rise of the Ayyubid dynasty, led by Salahuddin (Saladin), and their successful reconquest of significant territories from Crusader control.

The Ayyubid dynasty was founded by Salahuddin, a Kurdish Muslim military leader born in Tikrit, Iraq, in 1137 CE. Salahuddin rose to prominence as a trusted commander under the Zengid dynasty, which ruled over territories in the Levant, including Syria and Egypt.

In 1169 CE, Salahuddin was appointed as the vizier of Egypt by the Zengid ruler, Nur al-Din. However, after the death of Nur al-Din in 1174 CE, Salahuddin seized the opportunity to establish an independent Ayyubid state, which encompassed Egypt, Syria, and other nearby territories.

Salahuddin's reign marked a turning point in the struggle against the Crusader states. He united Muslim forces, rallied support from neighboring rulers, and initiated a series of campaigns to reconquer territories held by the Crusaders. His military successes and strategic brilliance earned him a place in history as one of the greatest Muslim leaders.

Salahuddin's most notable achievement came with the recapture of Jerusalem in 1187 CE. After a decisive victory against the Crusader forces led by Guy of Lusignan at the

Battle of Hattin, Salahuddin's forces entered Jerusalem peacefully, ensuring the safety of the city's inhabitants and granting religious freedom to Christians.

Salahuddin's magnanimous treatment of the defeated Crusaders contrasted with the previous sack of Jerusalem by the Crusaders in 1099 CE. His reputation as a chivalrous and honorable ruler spread throughout Europe and the Muslim world, earning him respect even among his adversaries.

After the capture of Jerusalem, Salahuddin sought to solidify his rule and establish a just and prosperous society. He initiated reforms aimed at promoting trade, encouraging agriculture, and improving the administration of his territories. His efforts contributed to a period of stability and prosperity, fostering cultural and intellectual growth.

Salahuddin's role in the Crusades and his reputation as a warrior-scholar have made him an enduring figure in history and literature. His chivalrous conduct, strategic genius, and devotion to Islam continue to inspire admiration and respect.

Although Salahuddin's legacy is often associated with his achievements in the reconquest of the Holy Land, his rule extended beyond the military realm. He sought to maintain harmony among different Muslim sects and fostered an atmosphere of religious tolerance and coexistence, allowing Christians and Jews to practice their faith under his rule.

The Ayyubid dynasty faced challenges from internal rivalries, succession disputes, and external pressures from other regional powers. After Salahuddin's death in 1193 CE, the dynasty experienced a period of fragmentation, with various Ayyubid successors ruling different parts of the empire.

The Ayyubid dynasty eventually gave way to the Mamluks, a slave-soldier class that rose to power in Egypt. The Mamluks established their rule and continued the fight against the Crusaders, culminating in the conquest of Acre in 1291 CE, which marked the end of Crusader presence in the Levant.

The Ayyubids left a lasting impact on the region. Their rule fostered a sense of unity among Muslims and revitalized Muslim resistance against the Crusader states. Their contributions to architecture, arts, and culture can be seen in the surviving Ayyubid structures and their patronage of scholars and intellectuals.

The legacy of the Ayyubids, particularly Salahuddin, continues to be celebrated and remembered in popular culture, literature, and historical accounts. His character, leadership, and achievements embody the ideals of chivalry, honor, and perseverance, making him an iconic figure in the history of the Islamic world and the struggle against the Crusaders.

The Mamluk Rule: Power Struggles and Stability

The Mamluks, a warrior-slave class, rose to power in Egypt in the 13th century CE and established a dynasty that ruled over Syria and Egypt for nearly three centuries. This chapter explores the Mamluk rule, focusing on the power struggles within the Mamluk elite, their achievements in governance, and the stability they brought to the region.

The Mamluks were originally slave soldiers, mostly of Turkic and Circassian origin, who were brought to Egypt by the Ayyubids. These soldiers were trained and educated in military tactics, administration, and Islamic culture. Over time, the Mamluks gained influence and gradually transformed into a ruling class.

The Mamluk Sultanate witnessed periods of both stability and internal power struggles. The political landscape was characterized by a complex system of patronage, where Mamluk sultans relied on the loyalty and support of powerful emirs (amirs) to maintain their rule. Emirs held significant military and administrative positions and often had their own private armies.

Power struggles and rivalries among the Mamluk emirs were common throughout the Mamluk period. Succession disputes, assassinations, and coups were frequent occurrences as emirs vied for influence and control over the sultanate. The sultans often had to navigate these intricate power dynamics to maintain stability and consolidate their authority.

Despite these challenges, the Mamluks managed to establish a relatively stable rule, ensuring the security and prosperity of their territories. The Mamluk sultans employed efficient administrative systems, including tax collection, land management, and the appointment of governors. These measures helped to maintain law and order and foster economic growth.

The Mamluks implemented effective military strategies to defend their territories from external threats. They successfully repelled Crusader attacks and fended off invasions by Mongol forces. The Mamluk military, renowned for its skilled cavalry and archers, played a crucial role in preserving the territorial integrity of Syria and Egypt.

Cairo, the capital of the Mamluk Sultanate, became a vibrant center of commerce, culture, and learning. The Mamluks patronized the arts and supported the development of Islamic scholarship. Prominent madrasas (educational institutions) were established, attracting scholars and students from across the Islamic world. These institutions fostered intellectual pursuits and contributed to the preservation and dissemination of knowledge.

The Mamluks also left a significant architectural legacy. They commissioned the construction of grand mosques, palaces, and public buildings, showcasing exquisite Islamic architecture. The Mamluk mosques, such as the Sultan Hassan Mosque and the Al-Rifa'i Mosque in Cairo, stand as testament to their architectural prowess and artistic sensibilities.

Trade flourished under Mamluk rule, with Cairo serving as a bustling hub for commerce between Europe, Asia, and

Africa. The Mamluks facilitated trade routes, established markets, and encouraged economic activities. This economic prosperity contributed to the cultural vibrancy of the region and attracted merchants, artisans, and scholars.

The Mamluks faced external challenges as well. Mongol invasions, particularly the devastating Mongol sack of Baghdad in 1258 CE, disrupted the region and posed a threat to Mamluk rule. However, the Mamluks successfully defended their territories, halting the Mongol advance and preserving their independence.

The end of the Mamluk Sultanate came with the rise of the Ottoman Empire. In 1517 CE, the Ottomans defeated the Mamluks in the Battle of Ridaniya and incorporated Syria and Egypt into their expanding empire. The Mamluks, however, left a lasting impact on the region's history, culture, and architecture.

The Mamluk period stands as a testament to the resilience and adaptability of the ruling elite. Despite internal power struggles, the Mamluks brought stability, prosperity, and cultural advancements to Syria and Egypt. Their military prowess, administrative systems, and patronage of arts and education contributed to the region's historical and cultural heritage.

Today, the architectural marvels of the Mamluk period, including mosques, madrasas, and mausoleums, stand as reminders of their legacy. The complex political dynamics of the Mamluk Sultanate continue to be studied and analyzed by historians, shedding light on the intricate balance of power and the challenges of governance during this period.

Ottoman Syria: Prosperity and Decline

The Ottoman Empire, one of the largest and longest-lasting empires in history, ruled over Syria for nearly four centuries, from the early 16th century to the early 20th century. This chapter delves into the period of Ottoman rule in Syria, highlighting its initial prosperity and subsequent decline.

The Ottoman Empire, led by Sultan Selim I, conquered Syria from the Mamluks in 1516 CE, incorporating it into their expanding empire. The Ottomans brought a centralized administration to the region, establishing provincial governance and implementing their own legal and economic systems.

During the early years of Ottoman rule, Syria experienced relative stability and economic prosperity. The empire's infrastructure projects, such as the construction of roads, bridges, and caravanserais, improved transportation and trade networks, bolstering economic activities. Major cities like Damascus, Aleppo, and Hama thrived as centers of commerce and cultural exchange.

Under Ottoman rule, Syria was divided into several administrative units, known as eyalets or vilayets, each governed by a pasha or beylerbey. These provincial governors were responsible for maintaining law and order, collecting taxes, and administering justice. Local notables, such as the urban elites and influential families, played a crucial role in the administration and governance of their respective regions.

The Ottoman Empire upheld Islamic law (Sharia) as the basis of the legal system in Syria. Islamic courts, known as qadis, were responsible for settling disputes and administering justice according to Islamic principles. The empire respected the religious diversity of the region, allowing non-Muslim communities, such as Christians and Jews, to practice their faith under the millet system, which granted them a degree of autonomy in religious and personal matters.

The Ottomans left a lasting architectural legacy in Syria. They commissioned the construction of mosques, palaces, and public buildings, blending Islamic and Ottoman architectural styles. Iconic structures, such as the Umayyad Mosque in Damascus and the Citadel of Aleppo, exemplify the grandeur and architectural achievements of Ottoman Syria.

Trade continued to flourish under Ottoman rule, with Syria serving as a vital hub connecting Europe, Asia, and Africa. The empire's control over strategic trade routes, such as the Silk Road and the spice trade, brought economic benefits to the region. Damascus, renowned for its skilled artisans and quality craftsmanship, became renowned for its silk production, textile manufacturing, and metalwork.

However, the later years of Ottoman rule witnessed a decline in Syria's prosperity. Economic stagnation, coupled with increasing external pressures and internal strife within the empire, had adverse effects on the region. The decline of long-distance trade routes, the disruption caused by European colonialism, and the Ottoman Empire's struggle to adapt to changing global dynamics all contributed to Syria's economic setbacks.

Moreover, the empire's centralization efforts and heavy tax burden on the population led to grievances and discontent among the local inhabitants. Revolts and uprisings erupted in various parts of Syria, reflecting a growing sense of frustration and desire for greater autonomy. The decline of the Ottoman Empire in the 19th century further weakened its hold over Syria. European powers, particularly France and Britain, sought to exert influence and control in the region. The empire's inability to effectively resist external pressures and its internal administrative challenges weakened its authority over Syria.

The latter half of the 19th century and early 20th century witnessed the rise of Arab nationalism and calls for independence from Ottoman rule. The Ottoman Empire's participation in World War I further contributed to its decline, as it sided with the Central Powers and faced military defeat.

In the aftermath of World War I, the Ottoman Empire collapsed, and Syria came under the mandate of France, as authorized by the League of Nations. The era of Ottoman rule in Syria had come to an end, leaving a complex legacy of both prosperity and decline.

The Ottoman period in Syria remains a subject of historical analysis and debate. Scholars continue to explore the economic, social, and cultural dynamics of this period, examining its impact on Syria's history and identity. The remnants of Ottoman architecture and cultural practices serve as reminders of this chapter in Syrian history, while the challenges and complexities faced by the empire shed light on the broader context of the decline of empires in the modern era.

Lawrence of Arabia and the Arab Revolt

The Arab Revolt, led by Lawrence of Arabia, stands as a remarkable episode in the history of Syria and the broader Middle East during World War I. This chapter explores the Arab Revolt, Lawrence's role in it, and its impact on the region.

T.E. Lawrence, also known as Lawrence of Arabia, was a British archaeologist, scholar, and military officer who played a significant role in the Arab Revolt. The revolt was an uprising of Arab tribes against the Ottoman Empire, with the goal of achieving independence and self-rule for Arab territories under Ottoman control.

Lawrence's involvement in the Arab Revolt began when he was assigned to the British intelligence services in Cairo, Egypt. His knowledge of the region, its people, and his fluency in Arabic made him a valuable asset in coordinating with Arab leaders and facilitating the revolt against the Ottomans.

Lawrence became an advisor and military strategist for the Arab forces led by Sherif Hussein, the Sharif of Mecca, and his sons. Lawrence's efforts aimed to unify and coordinate the Arab tribes, fostering a sense of common purpose and determination to achieve independence.

The Arab Revolt was ignited in June 1916 when Sherif Hussein declared a revolt against the Ottoman Empire. Arab forces, with Lawrence as a key liaison, conducted guerrilla warfare and launched successful attacks against

Ottoman garrisons, disrupting their control over strategic areas.

Lawrence's knowledge of the terrain and his understanding of Arab tribal dynamics proved instrumental in the success of the Arab Revolt. He led daring raids, organized supply lines, and provided crucial intelligence to the Arab forces. Lawrence's charisma, leadership, and cultural sensitivity helped forge alliances and inspire Arab fighters.

The Arab Revolt gained international attention, particularly with the publication of Lawrence's book, "Seven Pillars of Wisdom," which chronicled his experiences and the Arab struggle for independence. The book became a significant literary work and a symbol of the Arab Revolt's ideals of self-determination and freedom.

Despite the achievements of the Arab Revolt, its aspirations for a united and independent Arab state were not fully realized. The Sykes-Picot Agreement, a secret agreement between Britain and France, divided the Arab territories into spheres of influence, undermining the aspirations of the Arab nationalists.

After the end of World War I, the region witnessed the establishment of mandatory regimes, with Syria coming under French control. The dreams of Arab unity and self-rule were deferred, leading to disappointment and further struggles for independence in the subsequent decades.

The legacy of Lawrence of Arabia and the Arab Revolt remains a subject of fascination and debate. While some view Lawrence as a heroic figure who supported Arab aspirations, others criticize his role as a representative of British imperialism. The complexities of his motives, actions, and their long-term impact continue to be examined by historians.

The Arab Revolt, with Lawrence's involvement, ignited a sense of Arab nationalism and defiance against foreign domination. It became a symbol of Arab aspirations for independence and sovereignty, leaving an indelible mark on the collective memory and identity of the Arab world.

The Arab Revolt and Lawrence's role in it provide valuable insights into the complex dynamics of the Middle East during World War I. The aspirations for self-determination, the challenges of balancing conflicting interests, and the repercussions of external interventions all shaped the course of events and the subsequent struggles for independence in the region.

The Arab Revolt stands as a testament to the resilience, courage, and determination of the Arab peoples in their pursuit of freedom and independence, while Lawrence of Arabia's role, though complex and multifaceted, serves as a notable chapter in the history of the Arab world and its quest for self-determination.

Syria under French Mandate: Colonial Struggles

The period of the French Mandate in Syria, following the collapse of the Ottoman Empire, was a time of significant political, social, and economic transformations. This chapter explores the complexities and challenges of the French Mandate in Syria, examining the dynamics of colonial rule and the struggles faced by the Syrian population.

The French Mandate over Syria and Lebanon was established by the League of Nations in 1920, granting France administrative control and responsibility for the territories. The mandate system aimed to oversee the transition from Ottoman rule to self-governance, but it was met with resistance and discontent from the local population.

The French administration faced numerous challenges in Syria. Resistance movements, led by Syrian nationalists and activists, emerged to oppose French rule and assert the desire for independence. The Syrian National Congress, established in 1919, called for self-determination and an end to foreign domination.

The French authorities, seeking to maintain control, adopted a policy of divide and rule. They relied on local minority groups, such as the Alawites and Christians, as allies against the majority Sunni Muslim population. This approach further exacerbated sectarian tensions and contributed to societal divisions.

The French Mandate saw the implementation of policies aimed at assimilating Syrian society into French culture and governance. French institutions were established, and the French language was promoted in education and administration. These measures were met with resistance as many Syrians viewed them as attempts to erode their cultural identity and deny their right to self-determination.

The period under the French Mandate witnessed sporadic uprisings and acts of resistance. The Great Syrian Revolt, which lasted from 1925 to 1927, was a significant armed rebellion against French rule. Led by nationalist figures like Sultan Pasha al-Atrash and Fawzi al-Qawuqji, the revolt sought to liberate Syria from colonial control. However, the rebellion was ultimately suppressed by French military forces.

The French authorities employed a combination of military force, repression, and political maneuvering to maintain control over Syria. They established a repressive security apparatus and imposed martial law to quell dissent and suppress nationalist movements. Many nationalist leaders were exiled, imprisoned, or executed, further fueling resentment and resistance.

The French Mandate also had far-reaching economic implications for Syria. French colonial policies favored the interests of French settlers and companies, leading to the exploitation of local resources and stifling the development of local industries. The Syrian economy became increasingly dependent on agriculture, with French control over the land and agricultural production.

Efforts to modernize Syria's infrastructure and institutions were marred by a lack of genuine partnership between the

French administration and the local population. While some limited progress was made in areas such as education, healthcare, and urban planning, these developments were often seen as superficial and aimed at serving French interests rather than addressing the needs of the Syrian people.

The French Mandate came to an end with the achievement of Syrian independence in 1946. The struggle for independence and self-rule, marked by years of resistance and political mobilization, culminated in the establishment of the Syrian Arab Republic.

The legacy of the French Mandate in Syria remains a subject of debate and reflection. It is viewed by some as a period of colonial domination and suppression, while others recognize the complexities of the era, including attempts at modernization and the emergence of a nationalist consciousness.

The struggles faced by the Syrian people during the French Mandate played a significant role in shaping the country's modern history and national identity. The period under French rule serves as a reminder of the challenges faced by nations in their pursuit of independence and the enduring resilience of the Syrian people in the face of colonialism and foreign domination.

The end of the French Mandate marked the beginning of a new chapter in Syria's history, with the challenges and legacies of the colonial period continuing to influence the country's socio-political landscape in the years that followed.

Independence and the Founding of Modern Syria

The attainment of independence marked a significant turning point in the history of Syria, as the nation embarked on a journey of self-determination and the establishment of a modern state. This chapter explores the events and challenges surrounding the independence of Syria and the subsequent process of nation-building.

The drive for independence gained momentum following the end of World War I and the dissolution of the Ottoman Empire. The Arab territories, including Syria, harbored aspirations for self-rule and the creation of independent Arab states. The collapse of the Ottoman Empire provided an opportunity for these aspirations to materialize.

In 1918, the Arab Kingdom of Syria was declared by Faisal ibn Hussein, the son of Sharif Hussein of Mecca, who had played a significant role in the Arab Revolt against the Ottomans. However, the Arab Kingdom of Syria faced numerous challenges, including French opposition and the ambitions of other regional powers.

The Sykes-Picot Agreement, a secret agreement between Britain and France, divided the Arab territories into spheres of influence, with France assuming control over Syria. This led to a conflict between the aspirations of the Syrian people for independence and the French mandate authority.

The League of Nations officially granted France a mandate over Syria in 1920. However, the Syrian population vehemently opposed French rule, leading to a series of uprisings and resistance movements against colonial domination. The Syrian National Congress, formed in 1919, advocated for self-determination and the establishment of an independent Syrian state.

In 1925, the Great Syrian Revolt erupted, led by nationalist figures such as Sultan Pasha al-Atrash and Fawzi al-Qawuqji. The revolt aimed to end French control and achieve independence. Despite the determination and sacrifices of the rebels, the revolt was ultimately suppressed by French military forces.

Efforts to negotiate with the French authorities for greater autonomy and independence continued throughout the mandate period. These efforts included diplomatic appeals, legal challenges, and political maneuvering. However, the French mandate administration maintained a firm grip on power, often resorting to repression and military force to quell dissent.

The struggle for independence gained further momentum after World War II, with growing international support for decolonization. In 1945, as the war came to an end, the French authorities initiated negotiations with Syrian nationalist leaders. These negotiations resulted in the signing of the Treaty of Independence in 1946, granting Syria full sovereignty and the establishment of the Syrian Arab Republic.

Following independence, Syria faced numerous challenges in building a cohesive and stable nation. The process of nation-building involved the formulation of a constitution, the establishment of governmental institutions, and the consolidation of a national identity. The diverse religious, ethnic, and tribal groups within Syrian society posed challenges to unity and stability.

The early years of independence witnessed political and social transformations. Various political parties emerged, representing different ideologies and interests. These included Arab nationalist parties, socialist movements, and Islamic political organizations. The political landscape was characterized by a struggle for power and influence, with different factions vying for control and shaping the direction of the newly independent state.

The economy of independent Syria faced considerable challenges as well. The transition from a colonial economy to a self-sustaining one required efforts to develop local industries, promote agriculture, and foster trade. The government implemented policies aimed at economic growth and social welfare, but progress was hindered by limited resources, external pressures, and regional conflicts.

The founding years of modern Syria also witnessed efforts to define a national identity and forge a collective sense of belonging. This involved debates over language, culture, and historical narratives. The Arab nationalist discourse played a significant role in shaping the identity of the nation, emphasizing Arab unity, anti-imperialism, and the promotion of Arab cultural heritage.

Syria's independence and the subsequent process of nation-building set the stage for the country's modern history. The challenges faced during this period, including political instability, economic struggles, and the complexities of identity, continue to shape Syria's present-day realities.

The path to independence and the establishment of a modern state was marked by both achievements and setbacks. It represents the aspirations of the Syrian people for self-determination and the pursuit of a sovereign and prosperous nation. However, the legacy of colonial rule and the subsequent challenges of governance have posed ongoing difficulties in realizing the full potential of independent Syria.

The story of independence and the founding of modern Syria is a testament to the resilience, perseverance, and aspirations of the Syrian people to chart their own destiny and shape their own future. It is an ongoing journey, characterized by a complex interplay of historical, political, social, and economic factors that continue to shape the nation's path.

United Arab Republic and Political Transformations

The formation of the United Arab Republic (UAR) marked a significant period of political transformation in the history of Syria. This chapter delves into the establishment of the UAR, the dynamics of its governance, and the subsequent political developments that shaped Syria's trajectory.

The United Arab Republic was formed in 1958 as a political union between Syria and Egypt. The union was driven by the vision of Arab unity and the pursuit of a common Arab identity. It was a response to the prevailing sentiment of Arab nationalism, which sought to overcome divisions and forge a united front against external pressures.

The UAR was proclaimed by Syrian President Shukri al-Quwatli and Egyptian President Gamal Abdel Nasser, both influential figures in the Arab nationalist movement. The union aimed to create a single Arab state encompassing Syria and Egypt, with the hope of inspiring similar unions among other Arab nations.

The political structure of the UAR involved a centralized government headed by a President, initially held by Nasser. A series of political and institutional reforms were implemented to unify the administrative systems of both countries, including the merging of government ministries and the establishment of joint institutions.

The UAR pursued a socialist-oriented political and economic agenda, emphasizing state control over key industries and the redistribution of wealth. Land reforms were implemented to address issues of land ownership and inequality. These policies aimed to foster social justice and economic development within the framework of Arab socialism.

While the union initially enjoyed popular support and raised hopes for a stronger Arab collective, challenges and tensions emerged over time. The UAR faced internal power struggles, as well as resistance from factions that opposed the union. Regional and international dynamics also posed significant challenges to the sustainability of the union.

In 1961, the Syrian Ba'ath Party, a key political force in Syria, withdrew its support from the UAR, citing concerns over centralization of power and the erosion of Syrian sovereignty. The withdrawal of Syria from the UAR led to its dissolution, reverting Syria and Egypt to their separate political entities.

The end of the UAR marked a period of political realignments and transformations in Syria. The Ba'ath Party emerged as a prominent political force, advocating for Arab socialism, pan-Arab unity, and social justice. It played a crucial role in shaping Syria's political landscape for decades to come. In the years following the UAR, Syria witnessed a series of political changes and transitions. The Ba'ath Party came to power through a series of military coups in 1963 and established a one-party system. The party implemented a program of Arab socialism, nationalization of industries, and land reforms.

Throughout the latter half of the 20th century, Syria experienced fluctuations in its political landscape, including periods of authoritarian rule, political instability, and occasional economic challenges. The country navigated regional conflicts, such as the Arab-Israeli conflict and the Lebanese Civil War, which had significant implications for its internal dynamics. The rise of Hafez al-Assad to power in 1970 marked a new phase in Syria's political trajectory. Assad's presidency was characterized by a strong central government, consolidation of power, and the suppression of political opposition. His regime sought to maintain stability, assert Syrian interests regionally, and uphold a nationalist agenda.

In recent years, Syria has experienced significant political upheaval with the outbreak of the Syrian Civil War in 2011. The war has had profound consequences for the country, resulting in widespread devastation, displacement, and a complex web of local, regional, and international actors involved in the conflict.

The political transformations in Syria, including the UAR experiment, the rise of the Ba'ath Party, and subsequent periods of authoritarian rule, reflect the complexities and challenges of governance in the region. They also highlight the evolving nature of Syrian politics, the aspirations of its people, and the ongoing search for political stability and social progress.

The political landscape of Syria continues to evolve, shaped by internal and external factors, as the country navigates the challenges of post-conflict reconstruction and the pursuit of a sustainable political order. The future of Syria's political transformation remains uncertain, as the country seeks to rebuild and redefine its path forward in a rapidly changing regional and global context.

The Ba'ath Party and Hafez al-Assad's Rule

The Ba'ath Party and the rule of Hafez al-Assad played a significant role in shaping Syria's political landscape for several decades. This chapter explores the rise of the Ba'ath Party, the presidency of Hafez al-Assad, and the impact of their rule on Syria.

The Ba'ath Party, an Arab nationalist political party, was founded in Syria in the 1940s with the aim of promoting pan-Arab unity, social justice, and economic development. It emerged as a prominent force advocating for Arab socialism and anti-imperialism. The party's ideology resonated with many Syrians who sought a united Arab front and meaningful socio-economic reforms.

Hafez al-Assad, a member of the Ba'ath Party, rose to power in Syria through a military coup in 1970. Assad's presidency marked a significant turning point in the country's political trajectory. He implemented policies and instituted a governance style that would shape Syria for the next three decades.

Assad's presidency was characterized by a strong central government and a consolidation of power. He sought to maintain stability and security, which was particularly important given Syria's volatile regional environment and the country's diverse ethnic and religious makeup.

During his rule, Assad prioritized the Ba'ath Party's socialist agenda and pursued policies of state-led economic development. The government implemented land reforms, nationalized key industries, and invested in infrastructure projects, aiming to address socio-economic inequalities and promote a more equitable distribution of resources.

Under Assad's leadership, Syria also played an active role in regional politics. The country asserted its interests and pursued a policy of Arab nationalism and resistance against perceived external threats, particularly with regard to the Arab-Israeli conflict. Syria became a key player in the region, forging alliances with other Arab states and supporting various Palestinian and anti-Israeli resistance movements.

Assad's presidency was marked by a degree of political repression and a one-party system dominated by the Ba'ath Party. Political opposition and dissent were suppressed, with limited political freedoms and restrictions on civil society. The regime maintained tight control over the media and public discourse, seeking to consolidate its power and maintain stability.

During Assad's rule, Syria experienced relative stability and economic growth. The government invested in education and healthcare, resulting in improvements in literacy rates and healthcare access. Infrastructure development, such as the expansion of roads, telecommunications, and public services, contributed to the modernization of the country.

However, Assad's rule was also marked by allegations of human rights abuses and a lack of political pluralism. Dissent and opposition to the regime were met with repression, leading to a climate of fear and limited political participation. These practices, along with the consolidation of power within the Assad family, contributed to a system characterized by authoritarianism.

Hafez al-Assad's presidency came to an end with his death in 2000. His son, Bashar al-Assad, succeeded him as president, marking a continuation of the Assad family's rule in Syria. Bashar al-Assad faced significant challenges during his presidency, including the outbreak of the Syrian Civil War in 2011, which has had profound consequences for the country and its people.

The legacy of the Ba'ath Party and Hafez al-Assad's rule in Syria remains a subject of debate and analysis. While some view their leadership as a period of stability, economic development, and Arab nationalism, others criticize their authoritarian practices and the lack of political freedoms. The impact of their rule continues to reverberate in the ongoing conflicts and political transformations in Syria.

The Ba'ath Party and Hafez al-Assad's rule undoubtedly left a profound imprint on Syrian society, politics, and institutions. Their policies, governance style, and the challenges faced during their tenure have shaped Syria's contemporary realities and the struggles for political change and social justice in the country.

Contemporary Syria: Bashar al-Assad and the Arab Spring

The contemporary history of Syria is deeply intertwined with the presidency of Bashar al-Assad and the profound impact of the Arab Spring movement. This chapter explores the tenure of Bashar al-Assad and the complexities surrounding Syria's involvement in the Arab Spring.

Bashar al-Assad assumed the presidency of Syria in 2000 following the death of his father, Hafez al-Assad, who had ruled the country for nearly three decades. Bashar al-Assad initially represented a sense of hope and reform, with promises of political openness and economic development.

However, the outbreak of the Arab Spring in 2011 dramatically transformed the political landscape in Syria and posed significant challenges to the Assad regime. The Arab Spring was a wave of protests and uprisings across the Arab world, driven by demands for political reforms, social justice, and an end to authoritarian rule.

Inspired by the uprisings in Tunisia, Egypt, and other countries, Syrians took to the streets in peaceful demonstrations calling for political freedoms, an end to corruption, and socio-economic reforms. These protests initially started with demands for modest reforms but quickly escalated as the government responded with repression and violence.

The Assad regime's response to the protests was met with widespread condemnation as reports of human rights abuses, arbitrary arrests, and excessive use of force emerged. The situation rapidly deteriorated into a full-fledged armed conflict between the government and opposition groups, leading to a devastating and protracted civil war.

The Syrian Civil War has resulted in immense human suffering, with millions of people displaced, cities destroyed, and a humanitarian crisis of unprecedented scale. The conflict has drawn international attention and involvement, with regional and global powers backing different factions and pursuing their own interests in the region.

The Assad regime, supported by loyalist forces and international allies, has employed a range of military tactics to suppress opposition groups and regain control over contested territories. The conflict has been marked by the use of heavy artillery, aerial bombardments, sieges, and the displacement of civilian populations.

Opposition forces, including various rebel groups, Islamist factions, and Kurdish militias, have also been engaged in the conflict, resulting in a complex and fragmented landscape of actors with competing agendas. The rise of extremist groups, such as ISIS (Islamic State of Iraq and Syria), further complicated the situation and led to increased regional and international interventions.

The Syrian conflict has had far-reaching consequences for the region and beyond. It has exacerbated sectarian tensions, triggered a massive refugee crisis, and contributed to geopolitical shifts in the Middle East. The conflict has also highlighted the challenges of reaching a political resolution and the complexities of post-conflict reconstruction.

Efforts to find a political solution to the Syrian crisis have been challenging. Several rounds of international negotiations, including the Geneva peace talks, have been held with limited success. The international community remains divided on the best approach to resolving the conflict, leading to prolonged suffering for the Syrian people.

Throughout the conflict, Bashar al-Assad has remained in power, supported by loyalist forces and international allies, including Russia and Iran. His presidency has been characterized by an authoritarian and centralized rule, with limited political freedoms and restrictions on dissent.

The Assad regime has faced allegations of widespread human rights abuses, including the use of chemical weapons, torture, and arbitrary detention. These allegations have been documented by human rights organizations and investigated by international bodies.

The situation in Syria continues to evolve, with ongoing military operations, diplomatic efforts, and attempts at humanitarian aid and reconstruction. The road to a sustainable political resolution remains uncertain, with the future of Syria's governance, territorial integrity, and the rights of its diverse population still unresolved.

The contemporary history of Syria, marked by the tenure of Bashar al-Assad and the impact of the Arab Spring, is a complex narrative of political repression, violence, regional rivalries, and the profound suffering of the Syrian people. The ramifications of this period will shape the future of Syria and the wider Middle East for years to come.

Ancient Treasures: Animals of Syria

Syria's rich history encompasses not only human civilizations but also a diverse array of animal life that has roamed its lands for thousands of years. This chapter explores the ancient treasures of Syria's animal kingdom, highlighting the unique and fascinating creatures that have inhabited the region throughout history.

One notable animal species that has a long history in Syria is the Arabian oryx (Oryx leucoryx), a magnificent antelope known for its elegant horns and distinctive white coat. In ancient times, the Arabian oryx roamed freely across the Arabian Peninsula, including parts of modern-day Syria. However, due to habitat loss and overhunting, the species became locally extinct in the wild by the early 20th century. Efforts have been made to reintroduce the Arabian oryx to its native habitats, including protected areas in Syria.

Another remarkable species that has been historically present in Syria is the Syrian brown bear (Ursus arctos syriacus). This subspecies of brown bear is native to the region and has inhabited the mountainous areas of Syria for thousands of years. The Syrian brown bear is known for its robust size and thick fur, which provides insulation in the harsh winters of the region. While their population has declined due to habitat loss and hunting, conservation efforts are ongoing to protect this iconic species.

The Syrian wildcat (Felis lybica syriaca) is another notable animal that has called Syria home for centuries. This small wild feline is an ancestor of the domestic cat and is native to the Middle East, including Syria. The Syrian wildcat has adapted to various habitats, including forests and arid regions. Its distinctive coat and keen hunting abilities have made it a symbol of resilience in the face of changing landscapes.

The Euphrates softshell turtle (Rafetus euphraticus) is a unique and critically endangered species that historically inhabited the Euphrates River and its tributaries, including parts of Syria. These large turtles are characterized by their soft shells and broad heads. Due to habitat degradation, pollution, and overexploitation, the Euphrates softshell turtle is now on the brink of extinction. Conservation efforts are being undertaken to protect the remaining individuals and their habitats.

The Syrian jackal (Canis aureus syriacus) is a subspecies of the golden jackal that is native to the region. These cunning and adaptable canines have historically inhabited various ecosystems in Syria, including forests, deserts, and agricultural areas. They are known for their social behavior and remarkable vocalizations. Although they have faced habitat loss and persecution due to conflicts with humans, Syrian jackals continue to play an important ecological role in the region.

Syria is also home to a rich variety of bird species, both resident and migratory. The country's diverse habitats, including wetlands, forests, and deserts, attract numerous avian visitors throughout the year. Notable bird species include the Syrian woodpecker (Dendrocopos syriacus), the Palestine sunbird (Cinnyris osea), and the black-winged kite (Elanus caeruleus). These feathered inhabitants contribute to the ecological diversity and beauty of Syria's landscapes.

The landscapes of Syria have historically been home to a range of reptiles, including snakes, lizards, and tortoises. Species such as the blunt-nosed viper (Macrovipera lebetina), the ocellated skink (Chalcides ocellatus), and the Greek tortoise (Testudo graeca) can be found in various regions of Syria. These reptiles have adapted to different habitats and play important roles in the ecological balance of the country.

The ancient treasures of Syria's animal kingdom, spanning from the Arabian oryx to the Syrian brown bear, the Syrian wildcat, the Euphrates softshell turtle, the Syrian jackal, and a multitude of avian and reptilian species, are a testament to the biodiversity that has thrived in the region throughout millennia.

However, it is important to note that like many regions around the world, Syria's animal populations have faced numerous threats, including habitat loss, overhunting, pollution, and conflicts. These challenges highlight the need for conservation efforts, sustainable practices, and awareness to protect the diverse animal species that contribute to the ecological heritage of Syria.

Exploring Historic Sites: UNESCO World Heritage

Syria is a country rich in cultural and historical significance, boasting several UNESCO World Heritage sites that bear witness to its storied past. This chapter takes you on a journey to explore some of Syria's most remarkable and treasured UNESCO World Heritage sites, each representing a unique aspect of the country's historical and architectural heritage.

1. Ancient City of Damascus: The Old City of Damascus, dating back over 4,000 years, is a UNESCO World Heritage site and one of the oldest continuously inhabited cities in the world. It is renowned for its well-preserved historic architecture, including the Umayyad Mosque, an architectural masterpiece of the Islamic world.
2. Ancient City of Aleppo: Another UNESCO World Heritage site, the Ancient City of Aleppo, showcases a stunning fusion of architectural styles spanning various periods, from Hittite and Hellenistic to Byzantine and Islamic. The imposing Citadel of Aleppo, dating back to the 3rd millennium BCE, dominates the city's skyline.
3. Crac des Chevaliers and Qal'at Salah El-Din: Located in the western part of Syria, Crac des Chevaliers and Qal'at Salah El-Din are medieval castles that stand as testament to the architectural prowess of the Crusader and Islamic periods. These fortresses played significant roles in the conflicts between the Crusaders and Muslim forces.

4. Ancient City of Bosra: Situated in southern Syria, the Ancient City of Bosra showcases remarkable Roman and Byzantine architectural remains. The well-preserved Roman Theatre of Bosra, built in the 2nd century CE, is a remarkable example of Roman engineering and design.
5. Ancient City of Palmyra: Palmyra, once a prosperous city along the Silk Road, is home to fascinating ancient ruins that reflect the blend of Roman, Persian, and Arab influences. The monumental colonnade, the Temple of Bel, and the iconic Palmyra Theatre are among the notable sites in this UNESCO World Heritage site.
6. Ancient Villages of Northern Syria: This collective UNESCO World Heritage site comprises several villages in northern Syria, such as Serjilla, Al-Bara, and Qalb Lozeh, which offer a glimpse into the rural life and architectural heritage of Late Antiquity and the Byzantine era.
7. Ancient City of Apamea: Located northwest of Damascus, Apamea was once a thriving city of the Seleucid Empire. The vast archaeological site contains well-preserved Roman ruins, including a long colonnaded street known as the Great Colonnade.
8. Ancient City of Ugarit: Ugarit, an ancient port city on the Mediterranean coast, was a significant cultural and commercial center in the Late Bronze Age. Excavations at Ugarit have uncovered important texts written in the cuneiform script, shedding light on ancient history and culture.
9. Ancient City of Ebla: Ebla, an ancient kingdom that flourished in the 3rd millennium BCE, is known for its royal palace and extensive archives. The discovery of these archives provided valuable

insights into the political, economic, and cultural life of the ancient Near East.
10. Ancient City of Mari: Situated on the Euphrates River, the Ancient City of Mari was a prominent city-state during the Bronze Age. Its well-preserved ruins offer a glimpse into the political and social structures of the time.

These UNESCO World Heritage sites in Syria represent not only the architectural marvels of ancient civilizations but also bear witness to the diverse cultural and historical influences that have shaped the region. Exploring these sites is a journey back in time, providing invaluable insights into Syria's rich and multifaceted heritage. It is a testament to the importance of preserving and safeguarding these sites for future generations to appreciate and learn from the legacy of the past.

Iconic Cities: Damascus, Aleppo, and Homs

This chapter explores three iconic cities of Syria: Damascus, Aleppo, and Homs. Each of these cities holds a distinct place in Syria's history and represents unique facets of the country's cultural and architectural heritage. From ancient traditions to contemporary challenges, these cities have played significant roles in shaping the identity and narratives of Syria.

1. Damascus: Known as the "City of Jasmine," Damascus is one of the oldest continuously inhabited cities in the world, with a history dating back thousands of years. It has served as a crossroads of civilizations and a center of trade and culture. The Old City of Damascus, a UNESCO World Heritage site, is renowned for its architectural wonders, including the Umayyad Mosque, which houses the tomb of John the Baptist, and the vibrant Souq Al-Hamidiyah, a bustling marketplace. The city has witnessed the rise and fall of empires, from the Arameans and Romans to the Umayyads and Ottomans.
2. Aleppo: Situated in northern Syria, Aleppo is one of the oldest inhabited cities, with a history spanning over 8,000 years. It was a major hub along the Silk Road, connecting East and West and flourishing as a center of commerce and cultural exchange. The Ancient City of Aleppo, a UNESCO World Heritage site, showcases a rich architectural tapestry that encompasses Roman, Byzantine, and Islamic influences. The imposing Citadel of Aleppo,

perched atop a hill, has stood as a symbol of resilience throughout the city's history. Aleppo's traditional souqs, such as the historic Khan Al-Nahhasin and Khan Al-Saboun, offer a glimpse into the vibrant mercantile heritage of the city.

3. Homs: Located in western Syria, Homs has a history dating back to ancient times. It has been a significant center of trade and industry, known for its strategic location along major trade routes. Homs is home to historical landmarks such as the Khalid ibn al-Walid Mosque, named after the renowned Muslim military commander, and the Citadel of Homs, which reflects the city's ancient defensive architecture. In recent years, Homs has been deeply affected by the Syrian conflict, with the old city bearing the scars of devastation and ongoing efforts focused on reconstruction and rebuilding.

Each of these cities has faced its own set of challenges, including conflicts and periods of political instability. The Syrian conflict, which began in 2011, has particularly impacted Aleppo and Homs, leading to the destruction of architectural treasures and causing significant human suffering. These cities have become symbols of resilience, as their inhabitants strive to rebuild and preserve their cultural heritage.

The cities of Damascus, Aleppo, and Homs share a common thread in their ability to adapt and endure throughout history. They have witnessed the ebb and flow of civilizations, the rise and fall of empires, and the resilience of their inhabitants. Today, they stand as testaments to Syria's rich cultural and architectural legacy, reminding us of the importance of safeguarding and preserving these invaluable treasures for future generations.

While each city has its own unique character and challenges, their stories intertwine, reflecting the complexity and diversity of Syria as a whole. These cities represent not only physical spaces but also repositories of memory, cultural practices, and the aspirations of their people. They are places where the past meets the present, and where the spirit of resilience continues to inspire.

Palmyra: A Jewel of the Desert

Palmyra, known as "Tadmor" in Arabic, holds a special place in the history and cultural heritage of Syria. Located in the heart of the Syrian Desert, this ancient city has captivated visitors with its grandeur and unique architectural treasures. This chapter delves into the rich history, architectural splendor, and significance of Palmyra, shedding light on its importance as a jewel of the desert.

Historical Significance: Palmyra emerged as a prosperous city during the Hellenistic period and flourished as a vibrant trading hub along the Silk Road between the 1st century BCE and the 3rd century CE. It became a melting pot of cultures, influenced by various civilizations, including the Greeks, Romans, Persians, and Arab tribes. Its strategic location allowed it to control vital trade routes connecting the Roman Empire with the East.

Architectural Marvels: Palmyra is renowned for its magnificent architecture, blending elements of different cultures and exhibiting a unique Palmyrene style. The city's most iconic landmark is the Temple of Bel, dedicated to the Semitic god Bel and considered one of the most significant religious structures of the ancient world. Its grand colonnaded entrance, ornate reliefs, and intricately carved stone architecture stand as a testament to the skilled craftsmanship of the time.

The Great Colonnade: One of the defining features of Palmyra is the Great Colonnade, an impressive mile-long avenue lined with towering columns that connected the Temple of Bel with the western city gate. This monumental thoroughfare showcases the city's urban planning and the grandeur of its public spaces. Walking through the Great Colonnade, visitors can imagine the bustling life of the ancient city and appreciate the architectural mastery of its time.

Funerary Towers: Palmyra's necropolis is adorned with numerous funerary towers, known as "tower tombs," which were constructed to house the remains of prominent Palmyrene families. These tower tombs, often elaborately decorated with relief sculptures and inscriptions, reflect the social and cultural practices of Palmyrene society. They provide valuable insights into the funerary customs and beliefs of the time.

Queen Zenobia and the Palmyrene Empire: Palmyra reached the zenith of its power and influence during the reign of Queen Zenobia in the 3rd century CE. Zenobia, a skilled military leader and diplomat, declared independence from the Roman Empire and established the Palmyrene Empire, which briefly expanded its rule across parts of the Eastern Mediterranean. Zenobia's ambitious vision and leadership elevated Palmyra's status as a political and cultural force in the region.

Decline and Preservation: Palmyra's fortunes began to decline in the 3rd century CE when the Roman Emperor Aurelian reasserted control over the city, leading to its gradual decline as a major trading center. Over time, Palmyra faced successive waves of conquest and occupation by different empires, and its architectural splendors fell into ruin. However, the enduring ruins of Palmyra, despite the ravages of time and conflicts, have been recognized for their historical and cultural significance.

UNESCO World Heritage Site: The ancient city of Palmyra was designated as a UNESCO World Heritage site in 1980, recognizing its outstanding universal value and the need for its protection and preservation. The UNESCO listing highlights the significance of Palmyra as a cultural heritage site of exceptional importance, underscoring its global significance.

Destruction and Reconstruction Efforts: Unfortunately, Palmyra has faced significant damage and destruction in recent years due to the ongoing Syrian conflict. The ancient city fell under the control of various armed groups, and the world watched in horror as reports emerged of deliberate destruction of its architectural treasures. However, there have been concerted international efforts to document, preserve, and restore Palmyra's heritage, aiming to safeguard its legacy and promote the reconstruction of the damaged structures.

Palmyra remains a symbol of the resilience of human history and the enduring spirit of cultural heritage. Its once-thriving cityscape and architectural wonders continue to fascinate and inspire, despite the challenges faced over the centuries and the recent devastating conflicts. The allure of Palmyra lies not only in its physical structures but also in the stories it tells and the connections it fosters between the past and the present. Its status as a jewel of the desert serves as a reminder of the intrinsic value of cultural heritage and the importance of its preservation for future generations.

Syria Today: Challenges and Hopes for the Future

Syria today stands at a critical juncture in its history, grappling with numerous challenges while also holding onto hopes for a brighter future. This chapter examines the current situation in Syria, exploring the complexities and aspirations of its people amidst a backdrop of ongoing conflicts and the quest for stability and reconstruction. It takes a neutral, non-judgmental perspective, aiming to provide an understanding of the multifaceted dynamics shaping Syria's present and its potential trajectory moving forward.

Humanitarian Crisis: Syria has been mired in a protracted humanitarian crisis for over a decade. The ongoing conflict has resulted in massive internal displacement and forced millions of Syrians to seek refuge in neighboring countries and beyond. The humanitarian situation remains a pressing concern, with significant challenges in providing essential services, addressing the needs of vulnerable populations, and ensuring access to healthcare, education, and livelihood opportunities.

Political Fragmentation: The conflict in Syria has given rise to a complex political landscape marked by fragmentation and multiple actors with varying interests. The involvement of international powers, regional players, and non-state armed groups has further complicated the dynamics on the ground. Efforts to reach a political resolution have been challenging, with peace negotiations facing obstacles and divergent viewpoints.

Reconciliation and Reconstruction: Reconciliation and reconstruction are critical components for Syria's path towards stability and rebuilding shattered communities. The process of reconciling divided communities and healing the wounds of war is a monumental task. Reconstruction efforts, including rebuilding infrastructure and revitalizing the economy, are essential for addressing the immense physical and economic damage inflicted during the conflict.

International Involvement: The Syrian conflict has attracted significant international attention and involvement. Various countries have supported different actors, leading to complex geopolitical dynamics and proxy conflicts. The international community has played a role in diplomatic efforts, humanitarian assistance, and providing support for reconstruction and development. However, differing agendas and interests have posed challenges to achieving a unified approach to resolving the conflict.

Human Rights Concerns: The conflict in Syria has witnessed numerous human rights violations, including civilian casualties, displacement, arbitrary detentions, and restrictions on freedom of expression and assembly. Upholding human rights and ensuring accountability for these violations is crucial for achieving sustainable peace and justice. International organizations and human rights advocates continue to monitor the situation and advocate for the protection of human rights in Syria.

Socio-Economic Challenges: The Syrian economy has suffered severe setbacks due to the conflict, including the destruction of infrastructure, the loss of human capital, and disruptions to trade and investment. The challenge of rebuilding the economy and creating sustainable livelihoods is enormous. Reinvigorating agriculture, industry, and services sectors, as well as fostering job creation and attracting investment, are crucial for the country's recovery.

Refugee Crisis: The Syrian conflict has caused one of the largest refugee crises in recent history. Millions of Syrians have sought safety and refuge in neighboring countries and beyond, placing significant strain on host communities and international humanitarian systems. The challenges of addressing the needs of refugees, ensuring their protection, and facilitating safe and voluntary return or resettlement remain complex and multifaceted.

Civil Society and Grassroots Initiatives: Despite the challenges, Syrian civil society has demonstrated resilience and resourcefulness in responding to the needs of their communities. Grassroots initiatives have emerged, addressing various aspects of the humanitarian crisis and promoting social cohesion. Local organizations and individuals play a crucial role in providing humanitarian assistance, education, healthcare, and other essential services.

Hope for the Future: Amidst the challenges, there are glimpses of hope for a better future in Syria. The resilience and determination of the Syrian people, coupled with international support and efforts, offer the potential for positive change. Rebuilding communities, fostering reconciliation, promoting social cohesion, and investing in education and youth empowerment are essential for shaping a more inclusive and prosperous future.

International Support and Reconstruction Efforts: The international community plays a vital role in supporting

Syria's recovery and reconstruction. Donor conferences and humanitarian aid efforts are essential for meeting immediate needs and supporting long-term development. Balancing the humanitarian imperative with the imperative of accountability and justice is a complex task that requires careful coordination and collaboration.

Syria today faces significant challenges on multiple fronts, encompassing humanitarian, political, socio-economic, and human rights dimensions. However, amidst the complexities, there are opportunities for progress, reconciliation, and rebuilding. The road ahead may be arduous, requiring sustained commitment, dialogue, and collective action from all stakeholders. Ultimately, the hopes for a peaceful, inclusive, and prosperous Syria lie in the hands of its people, supported by the international community, as they navigate the path towards a better future.

Conclusion

The history of Syria is a tapestry woven with threads of ancient civilizations, diverse cultures, and a rich architectural heritage. From the rise of ancient cities and empires to the challenges faced in the modern era, Syria has experienced moments of glory and endured periods of turmoil. Throughout its history, the country has been a melting pot of cultures, influenced by various civilizations and serving as a crossroads for trade and cultural exchange.

Syria's historical narrative encompasses a wide array of civilizations, including the Arameans, Romans, Greeks, Persians, Byzantines, and Arabs, among others. These civilizations left indelible marks on the landscape, reflected in the remarkable architectural marvels and archaeological sites that dot the country. From the ancient city of Palmyra, a jewel of the desert, to the vibrant streets of Damascus and Aleppo, Syria's cultural heritage stands as a testament to the ingenuity, creativity, and resilience of its people.

However, Syria's history is not without its challenges. The country has experienced conflicts, conquests, and periods of political instability throughout the centuries. The impact of external powers and regional dynamics has often shaped its trajectory, leaving lasting imprints on its society and institutions. Recent decades have seen the Syrian people grappling with the consequences of armed conflicts, humanitarian crises, and displacement on an unprecedented scale. The toll on human lives and the devastation to infrastructure and cultural heritage have been significant.

Amidst these challenges, there is hope. The Syrian people have shown remarkable resilience, tenacity, and a desire for peace and stability. Efforts for reconciliation, reconstruction, and safeguarding cultural heritage have emerged from within Syrian society and garnered support from the international community. Civil society organizations, grassroots initiatives, and individuals have played a crucial role in addressing immediate needs, promoting social cohesion, and laying the foundations for a better future. Looking ahead, the path to a peaceful and prosperous Syria is complex. Reconciliation, political dialogue, and a commitment to human rights and justice are essential for healing the wounds of the past and fostering a more inclusive society. The preservation and restoration of cultural heritage, such as the UNESCO World Heritage sites, hold immense value in promoting national identity, fostering tourism, and contributing to social and economic development.

International support and collaboration are crucial in addressing the challenges facing Syria. Humanitarian assistance, sustainable development initiatives, and diplomatic efforts aimed at finding a political resolution are necessary components of a comprehensive approach. The international community, with its diverse stakeholders, can play a pivotal role in supporting Syria's aspirations for stability, reconstruction, and a brighter future.

As we conclude this journey through the history of Syria, it is important to recognize the complexity and depth of its historical narrative. Syria's past is a testament to the interconnectedness of civilizations, the resilience of its people, and the enduring value of cultural heritage. By understanding the lessons of history and embracing the shared aspirations for a peaceful and prosperous Syria, we can contribute to shaping a better future for this ancient land and its remarkable people.

Thank you for taking the time to read this book on the history of Syria. We hope that the journey through its rich past has been enlightening and captivating. Our aim was to provide you with an informative and engaging exploration of Syria's historical narrative, cultural heritage, and the challenges it faces today.

We would greatly appreciate it if you could take a moment to leave a positive review of the book. Your feedback is invaluable in helping us improve and reach a wider audience who may benefit from the knowledge and insights shared within these pages. Your review will not only encourage others to discover this book but also motivate us to continue creating content that educates and inspires.

Once again, thank you for your time and interest. We hope this book has left you with a deeper appreciation for the history and culture of Syria. Your support and feedback mean a great deal to us, and we look forward to sharing more enriching journeys through history and culture in the future.

Made in the USA
Las Vegas, NV
22 March 2025